ISBN 978-0-265-21527-2
PIBN 10223685

POT POURRI

OF

RHYTHMS AND PROSE.

By WILLIAM FURNISS.

"And what is friendship, but a name?
A charm that lulls to sleep ;
A *shade* that follows wealth or fame,
But leaves the *wretch* to weep!"

New York:

PUBLISHED BY THE AMERICAN NEWS CO.,

No. 123 Nassau Street.

1874.

To My Friends

THE STRIKER FAMILY,

OF

New York,

This Volume is Most Respectfully

Dedicated.

PREFACE.

INDIGNATION makes verses, and sometimes poets grow mad in writing poetry : and again " every thing is lovely, and the goose hangs high." The muse becomes at times very sick, and in soft affectation heaves a deep distress. Long-Fellows have been known to make short metres. We have heard of several scriblers who have died in the garret ; while others, like Ginks's Baby, have been drowned in a curdled stream of sour rhymes, We hope for better luck in the future of this Book of POT POURRI, which is a poem of a versical quadrature nature ; and that the critics may desist from their cruel censure and forbear the heavy blows of their fasces because of the author's attempt to be witty, which they have packed up in the four quarts of new wine in old bottles.

Ite capille. " Go it, ye cripples, and festina lente."

We cannot omit the expression of our sincere thanks for the aid which has been kindly furnished by two friends in preparing this work for the press. AUTHOR.

CONTENTS.

———◆———

"*MON REPOS.*"

A Legend of the Past.

 AIR BLOOMINGDALE, the loveliest village in the valley
That runs from Rosendale up unto Manhattanville,
Winding a length of beautiful indenture in its alley,
Including the bold fortress of the old powder magazine on Fort Hill,
Which still remains fresh in the park, in memory of the war of eighteen twelve,
And ever will be kept sacred on Evacuation Days, at least by some few
Bold old veterans of the noble Guard, though by others laid upon the shelf,
For their descendants will ever bear them in mind, and ring the curfew
Bell over their graves, for Patriots never die, and the grass will ever grow green.
The fame of WASHINGTON, the saviour of our country, will be preserved,
And the "McGowan's Pass" be visited, and be very well kept up, clean,
By all who still respect the ancients, for mummies have been well conserved.

A wooden crest of mound crowns the upland bluff, above Striker's Bay,
Where the noble Hudson, decked with the white canvas sails of
    schooners, is oft seen
From my bay windows, while my favorite hounds are at their play,
And the beds of flowers, grouped in banks of red, within a marginal
    of green,
Lying underneath the thorn, locust trees stand now deprived of leaves,
For the clear cold of Autumn, with November and blowing wind,
Have keenly stripped the chestnut trees, and cast their nuts out of
    their coaty rind,
Howling with the tempestuous roar of rushing force, to much remind
Of the distant throbbings of the ocean, as it swells along the naked
    coast,
With impulse breaking in white capped spray against the bolder rocks
    behind,
And shocks the breathless air with empty vapory frost-like ghost,
And flies away like phantom shades, that mock the bubbles breaking,
Like ravings of the deep despair which beats out on the seas,
And heaves with throbs of boisterous shrieks, partaking
Of those wails, and murmurs that move the heart in fantasies
That strike upon the soul with echoes from the forest notes.
In the deep bosom of the mountain's hidden lakes,
When light accords with music through the gorges floats,
To burst, to beat in sounds of rapture, of which the realms partake.
Thus lands and seas in one communion join to prove
That the God of Nature over all is the master at the helm,
And guides all creatures from His hands by love ;
That in all his purposes there will be forever room
To make provision for the human race and beasts,
If they submit in sweet submission to that heavenly boon
Which holds as well in great things as in the least.

Slowly glide the white canvas-spread sails of the sloops on the river;
From the banks I sit to watch these graceful moving barks—
The only poetical things that Miss Martineau chose to see in her
Last book on young America, written, perhaps, for the sake of some
    English sharks.
Silently they flit across the bosom of the majestic water's silver,
Like snow that falls awhile to be seen, then disappears as soon,
As any apparition, does that, disappears so suddenly,
As when a cloud is seen, floating light across the silver moon;
And the wild winds hurl their thin vapory forms as they are scudding by
These flock in numbers o'er the rolling, heaving tide-waters for gain,
Like the birds that rush southward in the fall, to escape the winter
    weather;
So float away towards the ocean-bound, for charter to obtain,
Or further bound, they wait awhile to shape their course on together.
And from the timbers in the forest whence they were first cut out
    from their rinds,
By the axes of the cutters, rent from the hills at the mountain sides,
These water-logs in wooden frames are but passengers on the winds,
To bear them to the goals for gain, where profit or loss abides.
They strike our fancies while we view their handsome forms,
Like the lithe images of some hidden mysteries in birth,
Torn, orphan'd stripped shapes of timbers from the mountain's oaken
    arms,
Which sky, and whispering winds through water bring forth from
    earth,
A full quartette of those wonderful works in man's human nature,
That do unfold the great resources of the Creator's master mind,
That sprang at first from out the grand chaotic creature;
That leaves the "Unknown Invisible" of the spirit far away behind,
And makes us to reflect that all that is revealed to mankind,

Is but the image of the GOD "our Father, the great I am," His word.
The Immortal bursting from the spontaneous mortal hind,
Whose world is an oyster which he must open with his sword.
The truth was well expressed by old Saint Denis of Spain :
"That it was easy enough to walk all round that ancient country
With his head under his arm and come safely back again ;"
But the only trouble was, the first fact that stood in the way, and
    always so contrary,
Is the same not patent in the present day to him who courts the
    muses,
Whose aim is only to amuse the people by his funny rhymes,
May he not have to bite his finger-nails, when he finds that the public
    refuses,
And turn in sadness back when they write him down as " behind the
    times."
But to wake up in sentiment : for a better subject let us now begin with
A verse from ancient, worthy Keble, one of Old England's saints,
And if one cannot succeed in making some folks grin,
Then all other lack of due success unto that end will be a want of
    paints,

       "Old friends, old scenes will lovlier be,
         As more of heaven in each we see ;
         Some softening gleam of love and prayer,
         Shall dawn on every cross and care."

Across the river on the opposite banks the Palisades in walls,
Throw up their bold and stony sides in gneiss or granite stone,
While villages adorn the crowning heights with waterfalls
That rush in madness headlong, wild in musical tones,
There *Tilly Tudlum* and her well wooded banks on one side
Look over to the long lines of meadows near the Pleasant Valley ;
And not far off that the lofty building of the Germans hide,

The spot called Guttenberg, from good lager when drank on occa
    sional rally.
Far off on distant heights stands historic old Fort Lee,
Recalling movements of George Washington and of memory's told ;
He was a noble patriot' and the Father of his Country,
While later writers state his boyish son was rather sold,
For neither the story of the hatchet nor of the original peachy tree
Holds any truth to carry its own weight in virgin gold ;
And this, like the " blarney stone" of the dear old Pilgrim's rock,
Or Pocahontas, John Smith's Indian gal, was a very bold
Draft on the imagination for the real facts to shock.
The Palisades in graceful lines of basaltic cliffs extends
Upward so far as The Tappan-zee, that noble bay-like sheet of water
That reaches beyond the ridge of Piermont, up to Nyack's bend,
Which checks our limit at the rocky hook as the halter,
Thence swings in revolutions of the rounding sweeping tide
That throws the channels back down to the lowest bluff.
Just at that point of the Elysian Fields, near Hoboken's pride
For all the Sunday pastimes, sports, for peoples' frolics ;
Nor yet forget the celebrated *Stevens* iron-clad steam battery,
That heavy plated monster, armed with mailed prows and barbs of
    steel,
So in preparation that in times of peace to sharpen up our armory,
To be ready when from all our enemies of foreign parts we an attack
    should feel
That the bold eagle of the American standard on the *ascutcheon*,
With its stars and stripes was not a " bird of brag and boast,"
But when it gets its feathers up, and fixed ammunition,
It was not afraid of Frenchmen or any British coast.
Thus much for buncombe and the inland scenery,
That lies behind the hills of Jersey flats and the lines of fields

That runs among the wild meadows and salt marshes up to Haver-
straw.

Now we will come back to scenes of graver note and worth in yields,

To speak of still life lying near to the centre of our own line,

That runs along the serpentine boulevard, this overturning of the
earth's old jaws,

That sprang from out the canny brains of men's red tape and twine,

Which, from meandering all along Broadway, streatches up to Harlem,

And if the river had not intervened would not have stopped at them,

There's no knowing where, but for the sudden death of Mr. Carman,

For these engineers of modern times beat the Indian chiefs at game
of ball ;

They fight to scalp a man because the big contractors cheat them,

And send their enemies without any scalps on head to Arabia the
blessed.

But for these nobby kings of Satan or Satelites of Saturn, but some-
thing of a dead beat,

For old Nick does lead them, and the sovereign of the daily presses.

The nearer the church is very apt to prove in them to be nearer the
devil,

Says a proverb ; so we now turn to the churches that stand.

St. Timothy's Church.

Between that church called Saint Timothy, the first to fight evil,

That this was first started in the lowest construction, like a caboose
on the land,

And was preached in a sort of log-cabin by texts from one Tracy,

A very nice fellow, who had a young Ambrose to help him,

With some clever old deacons, like Cushman and Striker the racy,

To intone with the people from prayer-book or join in the hymn.

Notwithstanding their efforts, this young priest did die on one day
From consumption, we learn from his parishioners and relatives
     dear ;
But we fear, if the truth must be told, he was love-sick, they say,
For we much fear that most divinity students think too much of the
     fair ;
What from views of themselves in the glass and carefully parting their
     hair,
They have always one eye for the ladies and another for prayer.
We have known a few who were dandies and rather given to dress,
And could tell some tales out of school of their pranks in distress.
But it is charity to cover these neophytes with a cloak of sweet love,
For I am sure the good angel above will wipe out such a sin with
     a blot ;
For which read in St. Paul, that all virtues are served up to prove
That old clothes and burned bodies of self, he cared not a jot,
Then turn over and mend, ye white-chokered priests, with your bows,
In low genuflections and loud hell-sounding frightful alarms,
And pound not your pulpits with anathema blows.
For all such predications, like the thunder, works surely no harm,
It is the lightning that strikes, which the wise man shuns ;
It is the silent still spirit of Faith, Prayer, and Trust,
That moves like the whispering of the sweet smiles of the sun ;
Like the dews of the morning that form jewels from dust,
And sparkle like diamonds with prismatic hues of colors,
Like our alms, which are the wings to lift up our prayers
To Heaven, who hears them in the blue silent hours,
For to relieve our burthens and drive away all our fears.

Saint Mary's Church.

THIS sweet thought we stole on a bright Sunday morning.
The time, it was Christmas, when the girls they were dressing
The fount at St. Mary's, with gay flowers adorning
The altar of the church, and so tenderly caressing
The noble old pastor, who has held up this church,
And stood manfully up to proclaim our salvation
From sin and destruction, without any terrible lurch.
In the vessel of sacrifice and of blood shed for the nation,
And through Winter and Summer he always was found,
Reading and praying and preaching from the Gospel,
The good tidings of blessing for the sinners all round—
For he cared for the poor and the rich man as well.
This doctor of souls was quite learned in geology,
For he published a book on " the recentness of creation ;"
But the writing of which did not disturb his theology,
For it proved that old Adam was the sole germ-sprout of the race ;
And all the rest of mankind, wherever a man has been found,
Was only a mixture of colors, black, red and white, if you please.
And development, like mushrooms or truffles, sprang out from the
　　　ground,
Was the mere offshoot of nature that was fanned by the breeze.
What with Huxley's and Darwin's, and other wise savants,
Who make men from monkies by the notion that looks at their tails.
For such we sent them to look at the wiser sand-black ants,
Or the oysters and sea nautilus, whose wings are their sails ;
Such nincompoops will never set the North River on fire,
Nor by "spontaneous combustion" draw off the white river Nile.

Whatever progress science gains by fisticuffs or satire
Will surely in the end from the wise provoke their smile,
A middle theme now sends to change the course of our rhymes.

Saint Michael's Church.

FOR shelter and retreat out the two former shrines or temples of fame,
Midway between Saint Timothy and Saint Mary's sacred limes,
Lies boldly, seeking notice from its fame has Saint Michael's name.
Whose "Legend of the Dragon" told about its fierce onslaught,
And victory claim'd from fighting with his majesty old Nick.
He fairly whipped the monster whom he stoutly fought,
And from the battle-field discharged him with a kick.
Now good Saint Michael's sanctuary has settled down in peace,
The present pastor of this shepherd's fold is shrewd and bold.
The founder was since a "Richmond left the field and gathered
    fleece "
From off the backs of sheep in former times, we are told ;
Until one bright night the steeple caught on fire,
And to the surprise of all the people, as they stood aghast and looked,
That there was scarcely a fragment left behind of the old spire,
That loss of the wooden framework arose from rusty stovepipe's heat.
Was but a gain, for he who followed next was born to preach,
When a bran new building from the ashes quickly rose in form so
    neat
That from the gothic shrine he could so much better teach
His gathered people in the congregation which he had to meet
The churchyard was not burned nor the soules that lie beneath,
In monumental tombs or graves covered with the green swards,

For these old parishioners had simply died from want of breath,
And in the resurrection hour will all have their due rewards ;
We will sing the song then of the bell that tolled so well,
For the hours of service as well as prayers within the tower,
For " the church bells beyond the stars heard, the souls blood ;
" The land of spices ; something understood,
Sounding with merry peals and of gladness for the bride so well,
As for the sad hour of the funerals passing power.
This edifice although built of wood was sprung with groined arches
In style ecclesiastic and lecturn of the proper antique style,
With windows opened towards the several aisles as stiff as starch.
Lighted with the chandeliers that are notched where the ·gas displaces
    oil.
So that the order is quite quaint, to suit the rubric of the prayer-book,
With bas-relief and other rare devices that please the people,
Who worship at their ease, although they should not look
Up to the Dutch shaped ram-like expounder, that tops the steeple,
The only exception to the general rule as to its architectural shape.
Say nothing of the queer addition, in a sort of student's telescope,
That looks as if the vestry had a quarrel about the money how to
    scrape,
And had to fill the *measure* by the piece before they broke.
But what's the difference in these revolutionary times.
When overturning everything as the new *order* of the day
With sects that vary in their divers creeds, and whims,
And bury faith in *superstructure* works of potter's clay,
Let us turn aside and see the fix they are in against *sin*
And all the tricks that Satan has to play, in *secret* hide
Behind the forms of Pharisaic pride and gilder's foil of tin.
Surely vanities were not *intended* for any church's pride,
When great Isaiah boldly warns " That without money's *price*,

Truly the LORD OUR GOD did never *intend* such salvation surely

We were to drink of the waters that were sweet and nice,

In order that the poor folks might hear the Gospel purely.

But prophets preach, the pulpits loud proclaim

That all the Scriptures are the birth-right of the poor,

So when the pews are paid for, this upsets their teaching,

For which Jesus Christ our Saviour opened the door,

That all the sly doctors who climb over the fence were peaching ;

He called them robbers who did fleece the sheep

And sold the wool from off their backs to sell

The skins as merchants do who filthy lucre keep.

Sheltered or sandwiched between two others, Saint Michael stands,

Sheltering Arms.

To hold the sheltering arms, the product of the good priest,

Who sacrificed his homestead to make an asylum for those infants,

Who lacked a cover for this charity exclusive of others, as a spot to rest.

It was named by a conclave of some clever kind of thinkers

Who borrowed the thought by suggestion from *George Law's* shelter

    cars

On the Eighth Avenue horse railroad, there were shelters sort of

    blinkers

To shield the passengers who were waiting and to warm their paws

In Winter time, when the snows fall and the winds were blinding

Their eyes, are likely to freeze their feet in the wet and cold,

And when you think of the analogy between cars and arms so finding

It was a spark of divinity for these wiseacres to strike before it was

    sold,

And the result was that the charitable building was left and selected

    out

As a holy house for the innocents, whose mother did not know much
    about their birth

Or, in other terms, it was a truth, that the parents could not keep them
    about,

The fact is these infants, when they are orphans, are a bother on the
    earth.

The truth is sad when we all know how German Müller

Built three goodly mansions all through the aid of prayer,

And when he began himself he was poor as any moth miller,

But his heavenly father heard him through the midnight air,

And the same was done by Baptist Knapp, a simple man of faith,

Who dared to stand on evidence in sincere trust and belief,

And took for text that Jesus was the guarantor of all the words he
    saith,

And those Christians who follow their Master are sure to find
    relief,

In these very words, it is written, " Open thy mouth wide,

And I will burst the gates of heaven to send abundant blessings

Upon thy stores and thy family that shall rush in like the tide,"

And the graces that will follow will be ever more refreshing,

For the humble shall be exalted when downfall goes with pride,

For Jesus is the Master, and heaven and earth are his own,

And he never will forsake the earnest petitioner on his knees,

For the Pharisee is a lesson and the Publican was better known,

And the good Lord is the giver, and bestows on whom he pleases

A further thought was just brought before the mindful muse,

That it was not the Poet's only object to astound the world

With studies of the churches, and book fill the Cloister of the Re-
    cluse,

And even fatted chickens only live to have their necks twirled.

But we forgot to mention two other temples on the main

Catholic and Methodist.

Road, and both in Bloomingdale, the one run by Father Brennan,
A Romish priest that came from Port Jervis, not from old Spain.
A venerable clever man, we know, if not, ask Patrick Brennan.
His post of duty is at the " Holy Church of Jesus " sure.
And, faith, I know it is so called, says Jimmy Ryan, his clark.
The other edifice, that has a Methodist to care, is not far from this
      holy priest's cure,
Stands on the hill, just back of the public school, near the park.
St. Luke's, the Methodist Episcopal, it is called by *Marks*, the
      preacher's name,
And Non-Conformists is the style of all the teachers of this mode
Of worship, for its all the same since Abram's and David's fame,
The secret talismanic key for entrance is " Let it be *a la mode*."
So long as it is the fashion for the rich to go to church,
And ritual is all the habit, and the style of motley wear,
The poor man must be hustled out with a snickering lurch
And has to do his praying and his preaching in the open air,
To that God the Lord of earth and sky and water also,
The Fermantal of the Triune Deity is doubtless three.
There will certainly no sex or sects be ever found in heaven we know,
For there cannot possibly be one God for you, another for me.
That would be an awful catastrophe for all mankind,
And the unkindest cut in any grand division,
To leave all the gentle sheep in black and all the goats behind,
Such chaos would upset the Mosaic code and call for a *revision*.

Bloomingdale.

Pass on to things unattempted yet in prose or verse do seem
To follow like a natural course of sprouts in the garden.

To speak now of the old past and the ring of boxwood green,

Laid out in regular plains not unlike the Plains of Arden,

In the ancient times when the Roger family resided here in glory,

So respected for their solid virtues and their Knickerbocker pride,

When they did drive to church in their four-in-hand, *the* old story.

Since that day's now past, but their descendants do not ride.

Those were times when Bloomingdale was quite like country,

And " King's Bridge" highway road ran like a crooked snake

Somewhat serpentine in form like the pond in Lake Glenmary.

Then the traveler to Spyten Duyvel did not ever need to quake,

In fear of hidden robbers by the wayside with his cocked pistol,

For all were rather poor and had such honesty of look

That no one thought his neighbor was hiding behind an ugly thistle ;

Or that a Will o' the Wisp of a ghost or a jack o' lantern light in a
     brook,

To shock the children in this innocent age by a falcon's frightful
     claws ;

As in these later days of modern ways we are left in Sleepy Hollow.

From what cause it arose except from some change of laws,

Like the Draconic code of ancient kings that melt away like tallow.

Sure these conversions turn in the history of some peoples' lives,

Are just as variable as the sun-flowers in their change of lines,

Although turning always with the sunshine it still survives,

Spite of head that bends all round as the orb of day declines.

These, like our watches, for every one claims that his own self

Particular time-piece keeps the time and is the very best,

And for the passing hour, boasts when he speaks for no one else,

For he deems that his alone is right, and wrong are all the rest.

For a man when convinced against his own stubborn will,

Will always remain of his own opinion still.

For it will be hard to kick against the thorny pricks,
As it ever was for a poor jackass to kick over a pile of bricks,

The Power of Prayer.

The churches banquet angels age,
God's breath in man returning to his birth,
The soul in paraphrase, the heart in pilgrimage,
The Christian's plumet sounding heaven and earth ;

George Herbert

That power of prayer was given to Müller for him to intercede
With God to grant his wish, and bring a blessing with it.
It was the voice of God by angels listening to his sigh in need,
And heard was the word of this simple-minded man, in spirit
He asked his father for daily food, and it was given indeed,
And heaven was opened as a door for what he asked,
For others, not himself alone ; at first he trembled on his knees,
And bending low laid his earnest supplication ; he was not tasked,
For our good Father of all the human kind is truly great,
And grand the store-house where he garners up the food
That not intended wholly for the sad beggars at the gate
Of the rich man, nor the hovel of the poor man, however rude.
He gives because the sinner's heart was faint and broken
With sufferings, and his tears and grief are as incense sent
From golden censors waived in viols as penitential tokens,
That all we have on earth was by heaven only lent
In trust for us to keep well garnished up with care,
That in return as sacrifice by faithful use denote
Our gratitude for favors granted through our prayers,
For " alms are the wings that bear our wishes to float
Towards heaven, who fosters all our thoughts serene.

If the donation is a meek oblation and sincere in truth,
So much the more is the seeker's wants requited if the gift is clean
And the heart beats in unison with love as in the vows of youth.

The Gardens.

What beauties lie beneath the well-sodded beds in the garden
     walks,
Dallying amid delightful banks of plants and flowers we view
The dark circle of the box-hedges that bound the rings in rigid
     stalks,
Then from the arbor turn at every point around the beds so new,
As if the hand had made a paradise on this earth below,
Where all that maiden's care and love of culture could contrive,
Was done to please the eye or charm the heart in joyous show,
And fascinate so well as to rivet the soul in this sweet life.
What gushing violets and bunches of daisies lift up their head
To fill the air with such odorous perfumed incense from the flowers,
We smell the fragrant jessamine and orange blossoms as we tread
And while the time in counting all these beauties by the hours,
As if they were all jewels in the crown that strew our pathway to the
     grave.
For I remember the fair Oceana, in thy love that decked these
     arbors,
Thy bright image still haunts the memory of this hallowed spot,
Thy voice, tho' silent, beats in the swellings of a hidden pulse, –
And thy presence sits beside me while thou art not forgot.
It lingers round the tulip-buds and wreaths of glory crowning us
With touches of a gentle hand that moves our soul, as friend
To friend in heart responds, as face to face in water does.
And we now wait long to fill thy place in the house of sweet repose,

And leaving all the meaner things behind to seek their real home,
In the mansion of the blessed, fresh beauties will disclose.
How all the rainbow colors that are seen in shadows here.
Will crown the glories of the endless distant shore.
And all the fantasies will be changed to substance there.
That Paradise is not far off to those that love the good,
That all thy fellow-men are angels sent from above,
That He who is all that is beautiful and true, alone could
Change all thy sweet songs of melody here to psalms of eternal
     praise,
As well he might create a new form of graceful creature,
And out of the mouldy dust another image of Jehovah raise.
For we will live forever and partake of a glorified future.
Wherever the flowers were planted the alleys were overgrown
By noble forest trees, that hung their graceful crowns with foliage,
So thick as not to shade the lovely green of the borderings sown
With ranks of everlasting forms of grace and noble age.
Among these walks the old man, like a nabob of the Indies,
Strove to while away the time until old age crept on,
By cherishing the homestead where he was born besides,
The greenhouse with the oranges and lemon trees to crown,
The patrimony of his fathers with his genial tastes of one
Whose pride was to improve and decorate the blooming dawn,
And foster with great care the treasures which not alone
Embellished all the landscape from late to early dawn.
The aged veteran strode along and view'd the groves o'er head,
The branching limbs of grand primeval stalking forms
Of oaks and walnuts, locust, beech, and thorn-trees, indeed,
And every variety of forest charm that man could farm.
This was a Paradise indeed, with pond and gold fishes,
Playing within the marble basin's round rim like a bowl,

Such as old Pliny would have chosen among his dishes,

With peacocks with brilliant eyes and iris shaded tails,

The bird that Juno loved, that ancient heathen goddess,

Who by the side of Jupiter, her husband, ever stood,

And ranked as Queen of Beauty, with her golden tresses ;

And, altogether, the whole mansions, with the primates good,

Were an assemblage of such uncommon attraction,

That if all the objects that could be brought together would

Form in one joint grand mass a compound of hospitality without
     detraction,

Not to be found on any other point this side of Hudson River,

For without exception, having travelled far and near,

The rest of all this planet were not really worth a stiver.

There was the resting place for the loved and dear,

Beyond the pleasure ground, standing erect in front of all

These garden prospects, is the large gold-fish pond.

It stands under the shadow of the ancient groves of tall

And noble elm trees, that bear a lofty mien above the entire
     grounds.

What with the ancient chairs outside, and library of books

That stood within the cases and the stock of valuable fixtures,

Including branching deer antlers and other things of a queer looks,

Such as conk shells of beautiful shape and some virtuoso mixtures,

The cottage by the river side, where the bold rocks on the shore

Form the barriers, like a bulwark to stay away the tides

Which rise and fall about here until they reach the nore

Of Sandy Hook or Neversink Light, where it hides.

This very ancient domicil was a feature to be noted,

From the fact that these landmarks of the islands of Manhattan

Will sink in a short time from the memory, to be quoted,

And will be lost to all so much as a man without a hat on.

A History.

So we will turn and swing our poem by a twisting of the road,
And run beyond this ancient bower of love and friend of mine,
And by a jump of many a stadia reach to where stood
Another ancient homestead of the days of " Auld lang Syne,"
That was called in the days ago the ancient Rogers' Place ;
Not Sir Coverly de Rogers, of the "flitch of bacon fame,"
But the father of the Kembles, another venerable race
Of men and women, for a rose by any other name smells all the same,
And if the smell of its fragrance is just as sweet to mind,
What is the difference between tweedle-dum and tweedle-dee in
    name.
Here was the residence of grandees, and the Knickerbockers kind—
A people who were somebody, who had pure blood, to be sure,
That had bodies ; but of souls, we say nothing more than they were
    kind,
For the healing of such diseased folks have the doctor for their cure ;
For of all races, as they follow down the branches of the tree,
Grow gradually less as they are distant from the stump.
To get at the measure of their quality its fair average must be,
Made of their degree in the mixture and be taken in a lump.
These old chatterboxes of society, with their nut-cracking teeth,
Are the sloppings over of a too full cup, you will find,
Forever gossiping about the stock of others in a sly under breath,
Quite do strain at their knats, but swallow their own camels never ;
The big beam that fills their hollow eyes—from the mote they are
    blind,
Like the mole that is always burrowing under the earth,
Which must be ferreted out by digging with a spade from behind ;
Or like mushrooms that rise up from the fog's early birth

To sink away when the sun is fully up in the sky.
These fossils of an ancient period of time quite forget ·
That the recentness of creation casts but a throw of the die.
These people own pedigrees, and are much like poor tenements to let
That this custom of antique folks resemble much the old tea-kettle,
They called the pot black because it had a darker skin,
Notwithstanding, these prejudices are hard still to settle.
Like their pride in the difference or distinction, is like a shadow very
     thin.
Leaving aside all such questions, as mere matters of dispute
For philosophy as well as of science, is of a very ancient date.

Origin of Title.

We will follow closer home by a new road to the farm,
And consider how the title of this history, now to relate :
A grand Mogul from the Indies came once upon a time,
For casting all his future horoscope through a teacup of dry leaves.
Crossing the threshold by a ferry, call it Atlantic or the clime,
He projected a plantation, like Jason, it turned out golden fleece.
By digging and good luck his works were blessed by the Lord,
Who has promised all his servants, if they keep honest and fair,
That they shall have full return and a glorious, rich reward,
Provided always that their dealings are on the level and the square.
Diligent in business, faithful, well he held on to his trust.
He purchased fields that many hundred rods in acres told ;
He felt assurance that, in time, to succeed he must ;
His qualities were strengthened by his ample bags of gold.
No ancient landmarks, by early fathers set, did he remove ;
No widow grieved, because her trusts held by him were broken.
Where she had confidence in his word once given that it was trove ;

For all his deeds and looks so kind, did ever so betoken,
His presence was a grace, and welcomed was every friend.
Such was the man who truly loved to greet his fellow men.
Strong was his faith in Providence, and faithful ever to the end ;
The poor man sought his door, the needy was not forsaken.
" Honor and fame from no condition rise ;
" ' The gold is but the guinea's stamp,' said Burns ;
" Act well your part, there all the virtue lies ;
" The man is a man for all that " he honestly earns.

The Farm.

Now on this farm there was everything to be found
In the old mansion of the good Roger family ;
His homestead was established well and amply bound,
It was well cultivated and cared for, with every facility ;
Plows and harrows, pigs, poultry, wagons and coaches,
Horses and carriages, even cock-loft with tons and plenty of hay,
Chickens and roosters, with henneries and cockroaches ;
And watch dogs with their kennels, and barn-yards for their full play,
Men who worked, and servants of all kinds and sexes ;
Those very *particular* Irishmen were not even neglected.
For there were trees on the places of every variety, which vexes
The man who trims, such as the oak, chestnut, locust, protected
With thorns ; besides sassafras, maples, walnut, hawthorn and beeches·
Again, tall willow and the tulip trees, which really please
All the fast ones who think of red lips, with the blush on the peaches,
Besides the cherry and white wood, that bends with the breeze,
Not forgetting the walnuts nor the ominous white birch,
Quite reminding one of our school days, when as school boys
We were taken by forcible entry, and taken across kness with a lurch

We were thrashed by the pedagogue for making such a noise,
Thus adding a chapter to perform the full condition
And fill up the catalogue of this nice produce farm
To completion, also overtask of faithful veneration,
Should omit some rare particulars and do it much harm.
It just happens, for my memory must surely be at fault,
How I forgot not to mention the favorite tree, apple ;
The Permain and Baldwin greenings and sour sweets.
The trees must forgive me, for the offence is so capital,
When we think of the cider, crab-apple flavor, that greets
And suggests the pure apple-jack, the sheet-lightning of Jersey,
Whoever has drank that will live to a good grey old age ;
I know that from evidence given me by one Mr. Hersey
Who served all his neighbors, for they thought it outrageous ;
Besides, what would Mistress Adam have thought of any such
An error on the poet's book, that in the part of Hamlet
He should have placed on one side this ancient Dutch,
And left in that memorable play the principal man out ;
Besides, Father Adam, first parent of all the human race,
Would have sought out the culprit on this blind occasion
And sent a token of his curses which might forever efface
This pure image of this sacred fact and spoil his whole narration
But never mind, the Lady Eve was generous and kind,
Too much chagrined by Adam's puling creatures,
Treatment, left on her vocative state, when she ran behind,
And left old Satan to console them in their fallen feature.

Sites and Designs.

PLAIN TALKS.

It is a wonder to the town that so near a great city,
A real country place may be still be seen at Sleepy Hollow,
Where primeval forest trees and boulder rocks in grand simplicity,
Afford a sheltering roof for the swiftly flying swallow.
Strange this may seem, yet stand the Woodlawn's groves,
Historic famous Claremont Halls rise high upon the Cliffs,
Where rushing floods of tides roars wild, like the rebel droves,
Its loud bellowing oxen, goaded on to market by drivers rough,
This surely shows that Bloomingdale, near Gotham city, is
But a syncope of ancient times and redolent with history.
That chairs exists since sixty-six with vouchers of all this,
And other remnants of the pleasant days are not a mystery.
The legendary stories of the sports are still fresh kept by some
Old antiquarian grandmothers, who will tell you by the hour
What belles they had been in former days, what beaux gave boquets,
How well they flirted with their fans, and jilted in their power ;
With many an evening spent at balls and mornings at croquets.
But we must hurry away from these, our sketches will not last,
There is some fun to lighten up views from these old sports,
And we hasten on to gather up the fragments which break cast
Of some clever jokes and picnics, walks, from these verses and their
    shots ;
Of Father Weber, an old man of eighty, we have a note about the
    Abbey,
Meinherr von Dutchman had a wife, besides he smoked his clay pipe,
His property ran down to the river but his stockings were shabby.
So in old age he took a woman helpmate of the young stripe ;

But as always happens, between January and May, he did die one day,
And all round the house there was an austere burial with hearse,
For the old man had married late, he said it once in play,
And as he bargained, so what he obtained, was some twins besides a
    nurse.
So this ends the first story of Meinherr and his glory.
The widow she departed, and after some consolation from friends,
The old Weber mansion was changed to an inn, with a second story.
But the landlord not keeping Sunday right, was struck by lightning
    and the fire burnt to both ends.

Reflections.

—" Mors est omnibus communis," writes a Latin poet.
A hearse is but another kind of stage, for all are carried by one to the
    grave.
So it occurred one day that every air-tight stove in parlors would
    show it.
How much resemblance to a tomb its looks so dumb and grave.
Another sweet suggestion arose while sitting all alone,
One day came to me on a bright fair Christmas morn—
Whispering, spoke the beauty of an Irish legend that had a silver
    tone.
It was that when a child was buried at a funeral in the island green,
The door of the troubled mourners' mansion was left open to the air,
It was thought that the angels might pass in and be seen ;
For these messengers are faithful lights, so gentle and so fair,
From grave to gay, from lively to severe, with gay return
To scenes of comic cast, and cheer brings joy to others.
Tony was a Welchman, Tony was a thief, but quite taciturn,
Tony came to my house and stole a chunk of beef.

Now this neighbor was an inn-keeper, his name was Jimmy Welch ;

He had a wife that plagued his life, and made him take to drink.

Now when a man drinks, the wine goes into the mouth, the wit to
the shelf.

Which is true that what one steals with the devil, it goes to the
brink.

So what money is made by deceit, over the shoulders of ill,

Goes out under the belly, deny then who can refute it !

For a dog that returns to his vomit finds it a hogshead of swill,

And it takes no prophet of wisdom or sense to dispute it.

The Welsh are but a specimen of many others in the past, we knew,

Them warning to deter their fellow-men from taking the first glass ;

A second taken may only learn how their *ale* to brew,

The last placed them on the road to ruin ; that people saw, alas !

Boulevard.

What a change has taken place in this region.

Once the people about here were social and neighbors at hand ;

There were hundreds of house-holders—aye, a legion,

And were responsible owners and proprietors of the land.

There were the Swains, Meyers, Malis, the Peunetts and Whites,

The Whitlocks, Le Roys, Van Post, and the Haydocks,

The McVickers and Sheffleins, Bryant and Browers at nights,

And Heywords and Palmers, the large owners of docks.

By some process of transfer, by the choice of better selection,

Most took up their luggage and crossed over the river.

In the wise ways of Providence we are told of election,

But it is somewhat hard for the rest of us to stay here and shiver.

That there is no accounting for tastes in this suffering world,

And we have to submit, for it is very wrong to complain,

For so long as garments are charged and buttons are twirled,

We have to bear losses as gains and endure well all the pain.

The blessings will come, one day you will see all this is right.

The Island of Manhattan carries a long body of two heads.

The crooked ways of this earthly paradise will surely be made
  straight,

And the triumph at last will result in a parable of gold threads,

The latter days of this seeming paradox but of solemn facts,

Will show a blessing for all those who will survive the change,

That the last spot on which the revolution in form reacts

Will show that between all extremes there is always a middle range.

And when the evolution of the present process moving

Will reach the summits and procure a finished end.

The lot of fortune will be thrown in the lap of patience proving

That he who holds on and keeps his purse holds on to his last friend,

Will see this island covered up with blessings for the poor.

The rich man may rejoice that he has placed his bonds on trust.

Keeps his wealth for future, he is not so very sure,

That Providence may before that day put his body in the dust.

The die is cast and not long to wait has he who serves

His Master first, which he has a very good chance below,

For he is loved who loves, and hopes for no return, deserves

A better fund of treasure from which he can bestow.

River-Side Drive.

These Boulevards are strange convulsions in the bowels of mother
  earth

That swing their huge length across the whole of Manhattan Island,

And hang a chain from Board of Commissioners of the Ring, that gave
  birth

To the grand idea of its transactions in the heads of sons of Ireland.
The longitude of its extremities extend in width seventy miles,
And they are all finished round the circuit of the spanded plan.
Its width would stretch one hundred and fifty feet by Deacon Giles'
New measuration, running from the reels in the stand.
Not quite content in beginning from out the Seventh Avenue,
The band of engineers ran up far over the Break-Neck Hill,
And plunging along by side of Dykeman's, from the last avenue,
Its snaky folds twisted over by Saint Nicholas past Jumel's
And coming back again swept past Bennett's and the Havens.
Having turned quite a somersault not far from the great high bridge,
And rapidly gerrymandering in a sweeping curve like thread twine,
It turned its graceful swan-like neck round along its summit's ridge,
Then ran a course in backward set in coming home near Harlem
    Lane,
Near to the line of the Six-Mile Trotting Park, just by McGowan's
    Pass.
From the control that guides its onward way quite near the powder
    magazine,
Then hides its head awhile somewhere behind the fence in grass
Thus, with contortions, extravaganzas, and extortions small and
    great,
Purposed by the first superintendent of this monster game, one Bill
    Tweed,
Proved but a new version of the Utopia, once by Sir Philip Sydney
    seen,
And through the cloud rising out of some very fragrant weed,
There rose a proscription by that master Comptroller, Mr. Green.
So that with taxes, assessments large, with improvements added,
The City of Manhattan will increase in splendor and in magnificent
    size,

And simple people will have only to hold their heads up while gaged,

For the glamor of a dream about the grand future had covered up
    their eyes

Including the Boulevards, well so-named from the French work,

From the fact that they have overturned every right of the owners to
    stop them,

We make mention of another construction called the Morning-Side
    Park,

Because the first sunrise is first seen from the side of the hill-top,
    when

The bright blush of its rosy light-beams peep over its walk,

This crowns the last ridges of the rocky height that look'd down on
    the valley,

And noteable in the time of the last war from the veterans who rose

Up in arms, with fierce valor, and bustled in hot haste to rally

And beat off all approach of the red coats by hard blows,

And we will finish off all this line of summary processes,

By the last undertaking of the crafty thieving of this cabal's chief,

In the route called by their fancy folks of the trotters and the press ;

Fast horsemen and jockies or turfmen and grand califf.

" *The River-Side Drive,*" which will run within sight of the river,

Always in honor of noble *Hendrick Hudson's* ship, before Fulton's
    time, who ran the first steamer,

Not like some of the modern boats that burst their boilers into
    shiver,

This plan struck one legislative Purserman, who was a good dreamer,

That it was of very little matter so long as he had his hands in

The city treasury, from aid of the pliant wool bags to pull all

A few more dollars from the rich men who were plethoric in skin.

For so long as the sheep are foolish, not brought up in their schooling

What harm was there in robbing them to get a little more fleece.

These geese were fat and wanted a goodly amount of pulling,

What cared they so long as they could stay at home to complot in
ease,

When primary meetings were distilling all the gin

Inside the bar-rooms of the publican and Tammany high-priests.

It could not hurt these innocents abroad much to sin

So long as they could brew a hogshead of headed beer with other
baker's yeast.

Memories of Things Omitted.

" One great and kindling thought may live,
When thrones are crumbling, and the memory of those who
Filled them obliterated : and like an undying flame
Illumine and quicken all future generations."

—Channing.

Some things seem small but still have the best of sacred uses,

Like the sweet germs of all the flowers that bursting from their roots,

Bear in their calyxun-folded forms, like oil in cruises.

These are but evolutions for their fully ripened fruits,

Their lives are hid unseen, but unfolding every hour.

What is the fruits but the true development of the stem

That is brought forth in revolving and turn round the flower

Untwisting while unravelling, revolves like the spindle in garments
hem,

As the light fingers turned the spinning wheel of old,

That spun the flax in harmony when maidens held the work,

To form the laces that wrought out fine filagrees in gold,

That float in graceful fairy-shapes like philacteries of the frost work,

To show the fact that angels' messengers from the outside world,

In fluttering visits to sprinkle the windows and brushing with their
wings.

Left the children of the snow storm while the winds were hurled,
And pattering steps tapped the glass in advent of the coming spring
Then winter came not as the burial of the covered earth,
Only to show how all things must bring forth a change,
That all terrestial objects are but the development of a better birth
And over all the heavenly hosts move in celestial range.

The Vegetable-Garden, Stables, and Barns.

" Too many cooks spoil the broth " may well be truly said
Of that sad poet who mixed up so many various things
In a compound of fancies that is hardly to be read,
Such as a curious medley of rythms and a satire about the rings
Among such a lot of fixtures as stables and ricketty old barns,
That stand between the first chapter and the finale at rest
To end in the good products of the dunghill and the fertile farm,
That are named in the catalogue as all of the very best,
Of vegetables to be placed by the cooks on any man's tables,
Consisting of prime potatoes and peach blossoms with eyes,
That are to take all the prizes at the *Institute's* stables,
Alongside of cabbages or cresses and ripe corn for the prize,
With asparagus and ockras and sharp rhubarb so tart,
As to spoil all the egg-plants and carots so sweet,
That all the blood beets turned quite red in the cart,
So ashamed were the parsnips that the celery had to retreat,
While the onions took to caressing the rutabago turnips
And embracing the pumpkins by clasping the vine
That the melons were determined to fairly water their lips,
At such a distortion of principles they had to decline,
So that all the committeemen had to consult on the case,
And concluded by rendering a verdict, a true one of course,

Now the jury was certainly out, but left in hot haste,

For fear that the expense of the trial would not reimburse,

They concluded, after dinner, by issuing a summary process,

By a writ of injunction, to settle the whole and check all the matter

Which was served by the sheriff, the result in the jail and duress.

The cook paid the costs and dished the kitchen stuff in a platter.

And to sum up the cause, she pitched the whole in a brown purèe,

And she told us, as one day she spoke from her place in her chat-
ter,

That in Irish woman's brogue, which she learned from Dundreary, by
the way,

A proverb, " *That the cook is never at shorts for herself when the Boss
has to pay.*"

Old Servants.

" A servant with this clause,
Makes drudgery divine,
Who sweeps a room as for thy laws,
Makes that and the action fine,
Whose eyes look up in faith."

She serves who waits, and waiting serves the hours of daily-need,

" Whose eyes look up in faith to see her mistress " well,

Shall reward her patience, a fit reward, from serving joy, a gift
indeed,"

Which shall repay all her labors from a fountain dell,

Which will flow from heaven with pure waters by buckets drawn,

To fill the soul, her soul, through all reproof of weather or spite of
thorn,

With trust in good, will shield her from the proud man's scorn,

And bring an angel in the early morn with his sword drawn,

To shield the faithful handmaid from sign of fear,

And watching over her hidden secret, humble line of duty,

Countenance her sweet submission and every toil and care,

To give assurance to her heart and crown her rest with beauty.

Such was the faith of one old maiden cook named Lucy,

Who passed her life in silent service to her heavenly father ;

She was formerly a princess, taken from the coast on Africa's shore,

And died at last in the brown cottage not much farther

Than fifty yards from the gate of her daily task of duty and grace,

That what was meet to complete the objects of her mission,

And was decently buried by the dear rector of Saint Mary's, whose face,

Much more meek than that of most of modern preachers, who lack submission.

Another ancient dame of venerable aspect and mien,

Was just as faithful in her walks, from the first day of this poem.

She was of Irish descent, and was born in the *green*—

For old Ireland was her birth place and earliest home ;

She was a crone in her ways, and quite prompt in her duties,

That no wayfaring fellow could approach to the gate

So long as this old Cerberus stood near with her shooties,

With all the dogs set upon these vagabond parties,

To send them away without food or paraties.

Thus her fame was well sounded abroad,

And the premises well guarded from without,

For shooting was expensive and murders played out,

And the angel of peace is the voice in a word,

And the shout of a female is enough with her shout ;

And the fort of a man is his own private *castle ;*

And Fortis in leges poteor in jure,"

Is the law of the Baron as well as the vassal,

And the screams of a woman is the yell of the furies.

The result of all this, there was peace in the house ;

And there's reason in all things, if we did but know it,

For the fact of the matter is that not even a mouse

Could be kept in this mansion so long as the poet

Of Bloomingdale lived there, with a cat for his friend ;

And you know that an empty traveler may whistle

Before the robber and his pistol—quotes Juvenal at the **end,**

And wooden guns stuck in the sand-bags, *bristles,*

Which are as alarming as the picket's sentry shout.

But to return to the aged female, now grown old,

She certainly knows well what she is about,

For there never was a more successful scold.

And we conclude with this secret for the ending

That what she did not know was not worth the while to **mind.**

Just like a message   by a fool's hand is not worth sending,

For you may still find another fool at the other end."

This moral finds this portion of our servant's tale.

If one wants friendship, never break your pledge ;

If you be very honest keep away from jail,

And never play with axes with a double edge.

Old Charley.

Have we forgotten thee, Old Charley?   Hamilton, thy other name,

Recalls a great *State* minister, who was shot by Aaron Burr.

Not to have remembered thee, old color'd friend, would have been a
    shame,

For thy services were constant, always ready, smart, and free from
    slur.

How often do we find that "like master, so is servant."

So imitative that it looks as if his very shadow followed,

As in the wake of a great rock, which the big pyramids in Sahara
casts aslant,

Where the shades of the ten thousand centuries look down, for I have
borrow'd

The grand Napoleonic Bonaparte idea, "his war in Egypt we can
recant.

Now this old nigger blackamore disliked to be called a black ;

Preferred much the name of color'd as best suited to his mind,

For his pride was as great as Lucifer—such reflection on the family
was a rack

Against his principals, whose treatment of them had been always kind.

He was a disciple of St. Philip's, was an attendant·at the church.

Now he was a staunch Episcopalian, and quite constant in his prayers,

His hymnals sweet. and his book of common ritual was a perch

On which he could hang his perfect faith to solace all his cares.

It was a feeling of great sympathy that bound them to his friend

Of all the color'd race, for he was surely one of the family of Adam.

There certainly was a negro in the ark, when ancient Noah did send

The boat afloat, well pitched, shut up in Gopher wood as tight as any
clam.

It has been proved in later days that Herodus was not a liar,

That one of the sons of Ham was not cursed among the rest ;

That Nimrod was a mighty one, and a credit to his sire,

And that the builder of great *Nineveh* was a man of woolly crest ;

And ever since the day of yore, and even to the present day,

It is told that the negro man was a great artificer in fire,

And he had a hand in forging out the potter's clay,

These casts of iron works from earthen pots that rise to higher.

It may be this man was worth his weight in gold in former times,

When men were chattels, held and let out as slaves for hire.

But things have changed since those days of barbarous crimes
Did rule the vassal's soul and spoil the serfs for mercenary desire.
The Lord has led captivity captive and given new gifts to man.
The man of peace has spread his fostering wings o'er earth,
And the angel has now risen in the shape of the pen ;
And the sword turned to plow-shares has given new birth,
For those offerings of Heaven to teach us that no being is so low
That the true law of its maker shall not in justice confirm
The full promise to the meek and the humble, the first right with love,
For all human creatures, of whatever climate and form.
It is alike in the tribute of equity and justice as their birth-right.
And that every submission in the bending of stiff necks
Make the easier yoke for the burthen to the back lighten.
If the load that is bore by the oxen, we are taught by the texts,
Is fastened by merciful hands of the loving master ;
They will move all the faster if the muzzle is loosened ;
And the end will be peaceful and the heart grow faster,
For the hand that is crushed hides the hand of the coward.
This old faithful servant at last gave out, and has passed away
To the *home* of the *aged ;* he was taken to rest for a little while
From his task of the body and his toil of the days,
And in the fullness of time, after making his peace in a smile,
He departed in the full assurance of the soul who prays,
That it may have these hopes of Heaven rewarded,   .
With the firm conviction that in the gathered harvest
He would have the measure of his faith awarded,
That he would reap what he had planted in the region of the blessed
He was buried with all the ceremony of the church which he served,
Among the faithful friends that waited at his burial,
And was attended by the friends whom he rewarded,
And laid his body in the Cypress Hill without further ceremony.

𝔓icni𝔔s.

From grave to gay, from lively to severe, we turn **away,**

And while the lamp of life holds out to burn, we **pass**

To other work and change the nature of the sad, to play

Among scenes of merriment and joyful mirth meet on the **grass.**

Favorable to health are the pastimes of modern times, we find

That picnies, or parties given out of doors, are often the most **agree**
  able ;

When pleasant friends assemble outside the parlors open doors,

To enjoy the sunshine and festivities held under the noble **trees,**
  when the table

Is laid out on the lawn, and the grass-plots form the needed floors ;

What with the dancing and flirtations under the trelliced arbors,

Mingled with the grouping of the croquet and archery, that noble
  game of the past,

The day passes always merrily until after the spent hours,

When the noon-day repast has been spread and gone, and the music
  last.

All the while there is running a rapid stream of agreeable interchange

Of civilities and conversation, and hospitalities extended to all the
  friends.

And traveled guest comes in to compare and swiftly run the range

Of all they saw in Switzerland—how they climed the Alps to their
  ends ;

And gave an account of all their little adventures and trips so strange.

Of how it happens frequently, that some old friend we see again, .

Who long ago we met at school and had our fun together,

Such chatting and gossiping between makes life appear a legerde-
  main ;

And it turns upon the constant thinking thoughts about the weather.

While some one will say whether it is best or not to drink your
    coffee
When its hot or cold ; some say it's tea, the others don't drink bohea.
Its all the same in Dutch, we say, just hand your tray to Cuffee ;
And if you like, a little more sugar, and perhaps a little of the green
    tea.
Then change to chocolate, and after slopping over a piece, take your
    plate,
And waiter—bring me if you please.   I'll take my cup upon my knee.
That's the *French* fashion, we are told, when the ice-cream is not first-
    rate.
And so the day goes, and everybody seems pleased to find themselves
    at ease.
Where everybody is in such good humor, who could ever quarrel,
For all good society is always on its very best behavior, sure.
For there was no concern whether your grey mare was black or sorrel,
So long as she had not the hippogippus, for that you cannot cure.
So well engaged that time passed away like a charm ;
There was nobody hurt, there was nobody to weep.
Miss Jones had her lover, and Mister Brown had her arm,
And all the old cronies cooed—all that they could warm
The inside of his copses, and the fine Havana cigars for outside ;
For the evening is coming on, and they are at a long distance, besides,
And a long ferry to cross, over the bridge there was a strong tide ;
But there is a carriage for Tompkins and a gig for the brides ;
There never was a party gotten up in such a grand style
Since the Baron of Bronxville married the splendid Miss Tilly Giles,
When they slaughtered ten oxen and roasted all the oysters in oil.
Then the chief was a foreigner and belonged to the Wildes.
In conclusion of all, that for picnics we have now to say in good is,
That variety was always pleasing, but constancy is not, I think, for me.

We have attended church picnics down in the Woodlawn Woods,
And at Mount Morris, near where the Sixth Avenue high farms—
That was given before Park enclosed the lines of this hill—
When the children went there to enjoy their fun and a nice swing.
And good Doctor Deems is pastor of the Church of the Strangers still.
He is a man after my heart, who seizes time on the wing.
But the picnic of all, that beats great and small for rare fun,
Is the one which one July was past by a Sunday School on the Bronx
River, near the farm of one Popham, near Scarsedale, in run
That leaves an impression on my mind like the seal of the onyx.
There was music and dancing, and swings hung on the trees,
Copenhagen, and caper, and carrolling, and heart's easing plants,
There were children, and cradles, and babes nursed on the knees.
But the grace that comes from this will comes back not aslant,
For the bright sunshine of love has gilded that prospect forever.
This was the gladness that gleams from, like the fullness of a river.
And the crown of that gay scene, I pray, will never sink,
For it beams like the moonbeams under clouds tinged with silver.

Charities—Leak and Watts' Asylums.

Now this good institution was in the care of good Mr. Guest ;
All the children—half orphans—were well treated and surely well fed
For the bread was kept over till it was old and sweet, for the best
Of wheat flour, well bolted and baked until it wed
That blissful state of digestion that leads to good health—
That waits upon appetite which comes from out-door
Exercises and gymnastics, romps, walks, within and without,
With plenty of sunshine, but not when the rain pours ;
But a good ventilation always keeps the ills out.
All the boys look so hearty and the girls are strong,

That, taken together, they grow up, in spite of all weather,
To make the best citizens that can ever be found ;
So that when they come to be men and women together
They were faithful and honestly formed, and be bound,
As a well twisted cord round a bundle of sticks.
In the fable of Æsop, where the man and his sons speak
Of the strong bond of Union that, united, will stand
Forever in friendship, so long as stars and stripes
Remain on the flag of the American land.
For the white and blue shield on the breast of our eagle
Will rise as still Excelsior, the foremost of all nations,
To protect all the people who hear the sound of our bugle,
And mingle their red blood as true common relations ;
Shall teach all the world that we are the offsprings
Of one eternal parent for all future ages,
And that to break this headstone of the fountain of springs
Will leave the sad destruction of his hard written pages.
So that the lesson to be learnt this year will show clearly
That peace will reign, because the day has broken
In no uncertain signs of glory in its glow,
And all the passed sunshine our future joys betoken.
This charity for orphans was founded by a fund left by two gentle.
    men
Of kind and simple natures, who had faith in the belief that to take
    good care of little folk,
Who had been bereft of parents, whether males or females, and de.
    prived of them,
Was to make them capable of being able to help themselves, without
    much talk ;
For " the least said, the soonest mended," is as true as " duty is to
    do "—

Something for other people, not for self—to stand shivering on the
    brink,

Just as one must first button up your gaiters and then fasten well your
    shoe.

We all recollect the fate of " Jink's Baby," who was left out with a
    think ;

For he came to grief at last, after all the society's fine discussions

About the manner of his disposing this thirteenth child of a father

Who had an intention of just throwing it into the bottom of the river
    Cruseon,

Thus to end all the trouble of providing for this infant without more
    bother ;

But the mother interposed, when the cruel parent thought to send
    him

To the convent care of nuns, with a ticket pinned upon his sleeves.

Up the spout of the elevator's gift box, and after ring of bell to leave
    him.

Such a proceeding was quite Catholic, and would save a world of
    grieves.

It was much better than to drown it, after fastening it with a brick,

And would have shorten'd all anxiety as to the fortune of the found-
    ling.

It would save the care of hospital and relieve the committee of some
    work,

And society would have suffered no great expense for the building

Of the supernumerary cradling of an infant, less so light as cork ;

But the kind Fates did order otherwise, and a good Providence
    stepped in,

And mercy lighted up a way for the protection of this lone orphan.

That was temporary relief, just as half a loaf cannot be sold for gin,

And the solemnity of the holy causes, at loss, proposed another safer
    plan—

To half educate this new offspring in the school about the origin
    of sin.

That Christians even may differ in their many divers sects,

But the trouble is too frail, a fact without any show of pretext.

My good brother, *Mr. Guest*, comes with the rest to close

The passages of this theme of household and homebred thoughts;

That seem to be given to me like the boquets of sweet roses,

Long hidden in the midst of a bunch of violet forget-me-nots.

What fairer binding could so well disclose the mind,

That folds within the secret of the silent moving past of years,

That were spent within the borders of this range of kind

Memories of friends, that stray over me like falling tears.

It may resemble more the dew-drop that slips between the jessamine
    and roses—

Like diamonds, sparkling with prismatic rays through lens of sight,

Those humid moistures of the soul in silent rests of hope reposed,

And wings its buoyant weight towards higher flight

Above the gloomy shadows that check its pregnant growth;

Aspiring ever as every happy form of earthly shape is taken

To reach the zenith of the prime of its ethereal worth;

It beats with heaving pulses in the progress that it makes

To fill up the measure and run its fuge in harmony of metre—

To beautify the birth that crowned it with such lustre,

And complete a perfect likeness to its outspring of feature—

That from the buds that were gushing forth to bind the cluster,

And fulfill the whole design in which it produce.

Just as the flagroots bear, in husky mould of earthly root,

The imperial emblem of the glorious Fleur de Luce.

These garments of the fields hold not a more gorgeous shoot,

Compared with all the lillies of the valley, do not shine.
For Solomon in all his glory was not like these arrayed.
The hand that made them beautiful was the Lord divine,
And human thought apart from *Him* has only strayed.

Old Lucy's Plate.

Knowledge is the treasury—discretion is the key to it ; it is power,
Some say, but wisdom keep, and you will reap your gain in the end.
But to maintain your youth hold on to temperance during every hour
Then frugality will regulate the passions and be your friend ;
While industry will be best illustrated by the bee-hive well stored,
Which the busy bee doth gather every time she sips the honey
From the flowers ; as she skips along among the yielding fields,
She fills her bags just as the merchant men their money.
But it is in self-denial that the most exalted pleasure yields,
The gold is hidden in the quartz-rock chasms in the mine,
And be quarried out by the Cornish pick and under heavy blasts,
And still the pure jewels of the metal need a process to refine,
To form the costly bracelet, that the fair arms of maidens clasp.
So we learn a lesson that Frugality is a fortune, and Industry a good
      state.
Now all this was taught, at my request, one day to bring a platter dish
Which old Aunt Lucy, kitchen cook, sent us for a porcelain plate,
Which was embellished all round, to illustrate the fish
Of pure morality, on which was wreathed all sorts of pretty sketches
Of trees and temples, castles, landscapes, rocks and running streams,
Cornucopia and date palms, bearing fruits alongside of foliage green,
And other water scenes, amid bunches of grass and ships. It seems
The letters round the borders were *Knowledge, Temperance,* and
      Industry, seen

Illustrated by the context of the bee-hive, with children's and women's
    heads and flowers,

To express the last, and then a flowing fountain, with a tutor with his
    scholars standing at his feet to learn

From Temperance, while Knowledge, with a globe and a ship in
    sight, teaching a youth under bowers,

That Knowledge, with Temperance and Frugality, would not serve a
    good turn.

And in the centre of this wonderful dish of human knowledge,

Were the elevated form of a noble palm tree, with mountain views and
    castle in sight.

The warts on one's fingers can be cured by potatoes, applied

In a poultice of starch, if there is strong faith in the bowl

Of good starch that is thickened, not if the touchstone is tried,

For there is only faith in odd numbers, said " Rory O'Moreill,"

When he dreamed of his luck, when he waked up one night,

To find that a nightmare had troubled his very vexed forehead ;

He was startled by visions so he prayed with all his might

That this phantom *hob*-goblin might be sent from his bed.

So it is asked that no pruning shall be thrown across this goose quill,

To stop the sad itch of writing from this table that will creak

Under the pressure of something that sticks out quite plain,

That had we only eaten a partridge instead of some hard quail.

It might seem then that the poet had a softening of the brain,

Which might cause a convulsion and make a complaint for the ail,

Or what would be worse than either, " The Leak or the *Watts*
    House,"

Bring another inmate of frenzy into that neighboring asylum,

That is called by the patients a good mansion for the carouse.

What *Adolphe Karr* insists on, it is a wonder that sound folks,

Should build such fine castles or buildings in brown stone,

That looks as if they were to make them on some practical jokes,

In order to keep the real crazy madmen outside on the curbstone.

For it really seems all the rich brokers have grown older in crimes,

And that stealing and robbing are merely some newly found gifts,

Sent down by the lightning rods and fastened with red twines ;

And that all speculators are quite handsome as true lifts,

That by their petards are hoisted up by a better kind of blocks,

To raise the wind by a kiting up through the spheres,

And that idolatry and mammon worship is simply only stocks

Of wooden presents saved out of the fires to be presented at the quin-
    tal years,

Just as a bridegroom does to his lady, when he is lucky if he lives

To see the fifth night anniversary of his wedding, provided always he
    survives.

Knowledge is the treasury and discretion the key to open its hives,

Well kept is the wisdom which is kept to foster your gains in your
    sleeves,

That will maintain your youth and live with happiness and in peace
    on his strives.

It was the bold Argonaut sailor, who won the golden fleece.

It regulates the passions and keeps you from sin and sorrow, quiet
    from thieves,

And in self-denial is the most exalted pleasure found in peace,

While industry is best illustrated in the garden by a bee-hive store,

That busy insect that gathers honey all the day from every flower.

For there can be no sufficient gain without much pain any more.

Like the practice of the French physician told his patient in the side
    hour,

Quit medicine and study, and throw physic to the drains ;

For frugality is a fortune, and industry will procure you a very good
    state,

So that you may live all the rest of your life without pains,
Free from neuralgia and heartaches, which might trouble your pate.

Prospect Looking Round Bloomingdale.

As when the traveler in a storm looks forward to the end of his
journey,
And sees the light gleaming out of the windows of his own house it
lessens the way ;
His heart revives, and strong with the thoughts of home he travels
easy ;
He breasts the snows and buffeting the winds, thinks it all fair play.
So does a writer who begins to write of things familiar from his boy-
hood,
Thinks it long until he seems to feel that the end is not far off,
And often flatters he would like to stop his Pegasus if he well could,
But deems it further ahead, like the mile-stone that seems to scoff
His weary waiting for the termination of the ever shifting sign-board.
This is so in a country where the roads are rough ; but now we are at
home.
The day of his years are passing swiftly and feel as if a long goad
Was pricking us behind, and that we have no longer ways to roam.
What shall we say of all the things that crowd around these pages ;
Of the quails we have shot on the old farm ground and the woodcocks
in the corn.
They have gone, and the singing birds have flown before the guns
of new gages.
The rabbit, that once dwelt in safety along the edges of the running
waters' tide,
Have, with the timid hare, been driven away before the progress of
the day ;

The cottages still linger in the old abode, standing by the wayside ;

Think they must soon depart, they feel the inroads of the money mart.

The old Rock Cottage, with its whitewashed walls, speaks of the blind man,

Whose eyes were struck out by the fearful blasts of powder, yet still do smart.

He had no redress for the pain endured, for he himself did hold the can ;

His family has never suffered, for the heart felt a sympathy for such a grief ;

And simple faith and work, with charity from friends, soon sent him aid.

And we have the locomotive steam stone rollers running along the road-bed.

There is scarcely one cottage family left but Thomas Farrar's, people say,

And omnibus and loaded wagons rattle over the gray Tilford rocks enough to raise the dead,

And the railroad cars have long stopped to land us at the dock near Stryker's Bay ;

And the churches are, except St. Michael's, looking up for keeps ;

The farmers all are selling out and turning out from their household beams,

To seek their fortunes for their products as far as Oyster Bay heaps.

Ten thousand changes have come over the spirit of our dreams.

The old have left, the new old-folks seem to dwell strange and wide apart.

And all the houses of the first owners or their tenants gaunt.

Society, between the running of daily stages, is bound daily for the mart,

And no one knows about his neighbors who do not leave the haunt.

The barrooms are increased, and the clubs so few and far between
  in round,
That the signs are not painted fresh from the absence of repeated
  calls.
Who can find relief in all the dwellers of the city more easily found,
Without the expense of carriage hire, from the convenience of the
  meters walls ?
When gas was given here it was only meant for the street lamp's
  ground,
But one favored citizen found us without one day in a corner of
  darkness,
And brought the metre up as far as the life of the nearest garden gate ;
So thankful are we for all favors had, from one Supervisor friend's re-
  dress,
We hope some day to recompense him, when we hope it won't be too
  late.
There is one peculiar fact omitted, which is uncommon to the univer-
  sal whole
Families of the human race, which is, that funerals have taken place in
  front of our doors,
When the Angels of Death entered the mansion and stole irresistably
  away.
Quite recently two burial cases, which are now covered with the
  snow,
In other years two others were placed in the same cemetery within
  the same days,
So now there are four that sleep together in the same tomb at Trini-
  ty's ground,
Where their bodies are still laying with the same grave-yard they laid,
Whence they will rest till the resurrection, when the trumpet shall
  sound.

And these dead shall surely come to life again, and be quickened in-
    deed ;

For we are convinced by the rising of our own dear Lord from the
    tomb.

For death is not the gloomy mystery, but the dawn of thy birth is the
    glory of heaven indeed,

And this fact was well witness'd by the Angels, that sealed this birth
    in the womb.

How the Lord had declared it—when he rose we were born,

And the image of Death is a crown of jewels in glory and gold ;

We, children of Heaven, were forced to be blessed. For all good is
    corn,

And without the impress and seal of a Bread that is leaven and bliss,

And the seed of the martyrs who died sown in their blood,

Clear'd the church of much fog, and sets this truth with a kiss.

       " Old friends, old scenes, will lovelier be,

           As more of Heaven in each we see ;

           Some softening gleam of love and prayer,

           Shall dawn on every cross and care."—*Keble.*

LECTURE ON

SPRINGS & FOUNTAINS.

————◆————

INCE the time when Light first burst effulgent from the realms of chaos, and life and animation from the depths of Erebus, mankind have yielded a spontaneous and superstitious adoration to the mystic charms of lakes, rivers, rills, and fountains.

The ancients believed the Earth to be an extended plain, with a mighty river flowing around it. This broad and deep current they called Oceanus or the Ocean, of which the overflowing Nile was supposed to be a part.

On the bank of this River were located the abodes of the dead, the islands of the blessed, and westward, in particular the sweet fields of Elysium, fanned by gentle zephyrs.

The sun, moon and stars were supposed to have their habitation in these waters, both to rise and set in the same, and to leave their abode temporarily to minister to the wants of man.

As the sun was found to be the genial source of light
and heat, and the moon of moisture, giving life to vegeta-
tion, these two objects were soon worshiped in Egypt,
under the name of Osiris and Isis. The one was granting
life and heat by his flaming rays to all, the other as the
nourishing mother of all.

Among the early Greeks, too, the salutary and benefi-
cent powers of Nature were thus personified to such a
degree, that in all the phenomena of ordinary nature
they fancied they saw some manifestation of the Deity.
Hence springs, rivers, and all waters, as well as living
vegetables, became the embodiment of so many divine
agents, and accordingly were peopled with *Nymphs*
almost innumerable, but yet of different orders.

These Nymphs were thought to be endowed with pro-
phetic powers, to inspire men with the same, to confer
upon them the gift of poetry, and ability to heal a great
variety of diseases.

It will be the object of this Lecture to point out some
of the more remarkable waters, medicinal and otherwise,
in time past, connected as they have been with the
observations and superstitions of mankind.

Early historians relate that about Tarbelli, a town in
Guinne, or Bayonne in France, and also in the Pyrenean
hills, that springs both hot and cold were found to boil
up so near together, that there seemed to be no distance
between them ; that other places yielded waters, com-
fortably warm and suitable for the cure of many diseases,
as if (continues the historian) nature had set them apart

for the good of man only, and no other living creature beside.

To these fountains, so medicinal, there was ascribed some divine power, inasmuch as they gave names unto sundry gods and goddesses, also to such cities as Puteoli, Aurelia, Aquensis, Callidae Fontes-Aquae Sextiae, and others. But in no country were found springs more celebrated than in the Vale of Bajanus, in the realm of Naples, where there were some charged with sulphur, others with alum, some issuing from veins of salt, others yielding nitre, some evolving bitumen, and others both acid and saline.

Here was the Fountain of Posideanus, so hot as to cook viands for the table. Here, too, were the famous Licinian Springs, boiling up beautifully from underneath the sea. These several springs, we are informed, were sovereign remedies for the infirmities of the sinews, for gout in the feet, for rheumatism, dislocation of joints, fractures of bones, dyspepsia, healing of wounds and ulcers, as well as for the accidents of the head and ears.

But among the most distinguished of these springs were those bearing the name of Cicero, called *Ciceroni-anæ;* possessing extraordinary properties for clearing the sight, and enlightening the eyes.

It was here on the sea side, on the great road leading from Lake Avernus to Puteoli, that Cicero built his summer-house and study in a most beautiful grove. This beautiful villa he adorned with galleries, porches, walks, and alleys, and named it Academia, in memory of the Academia of Plato, on the River Cephisus, **six stadia** from Athens.

It was here that Cicero wrote his books entitled · " Academia *Quaestionus*," and caused his own sepulchre to be built, thereby modestly declaring to the wor'd, that he did not expect immortality from his writings. ·

On the death of Cicero, this lovely estate came into possession of Antistius Vetus, a nobleman of Rome, and suddenly after his decease, in front of, his late residence, the above hot fountains, so healthful to the eyes, *burst forth*, as was supposed by divine agency.

On the occurrence of this marvellous event, Laurea Tullus, who had been a slave of Cicero, but at length received his freedom, in affection to his late master, struck as' it were by the inspiration of the divinity or nymph of the fountain, composed the following beautiful lines, which were legibly engraved on a Tablet set **up** over the Springs.

> Quo tua Romanæ vindex clarissima linguæ
> Sylva loco melius, surgere jussa viret
> Atque Academiæ celebratam nomine villam.
> Nunc reparat cultus sub potiore Vetus.
> Hic etiam apparent lymphæ non ante repertæ.
> Lanquida quæ infuso lumina rore levant :
> Nimirum locus ipse sui Ciceronis honori
> Hoc dedit, hac fontes cum patefecit ope
> Ut quoniam totium legitur sine fine per Orbem
> Sint plures oculis quæ medeantur aquæ." ,

"O Prince of Roman Eloquence, lo! here thy grove in place,
  How green it is where planted first it was to grow apace.
  And Vetus now, who holds thy house, fair Academia hight,
  Spares for no cost, but it maintains and keeps in better plight;
  Of late also fresh fountains here broke forth out of the ground,
  Most wholesome to bathe sore eyes, which erst were never found.
  These helpful springs the soil no doubt presenting to our view,
  To Cicero, her ancient lord, hath done this honor due,
  That since his books throughout the world are read by many a
      wight,
  More waters still may clear their eyes and cure defective sight."

In Campania the fountains of Sinuessa cured men of lunacy and madness, and in the volcanic island of Aenaria (now Ischia), there existed a spring of such acid qualities as actually to dissolve stone in the bladder, and another very cold spring, possessing the same properties, was resorted to for the same purpose in the country of the Sidicins, four miles from Teanum. Those who drank of the water of Lake Velinus experienced the same effect.

Varro mentions a spring of this virtue at the foot of Mount Taurus and Calimachus, a river of the same operation in Phrygia, but of the waters of this river, if patients drank over a certain quantity, they were driven to madness.

Ctesias reports the same of the Red fountain in Ethiopia.

The tepid waters near Rome, called Albulæ, healed wounds, and the very cold springs among the Sabines, called cutilæ, were remarkable for purifying the blood and giving tone to the system. Varro again reports that Titius Lord Praetor was cured of the loathsome disease, leprosy, by bathing in the Lake Alphion. We learn from a letter written by Cassius the Parmezan to Mark Anthony, that the river Cydnus in Cilicia was very effectual in curing the gout, while the waters about Troezan on the Saronic Gulf, were sure to produce gout and other diseases of the feet.

Cicero, in his Admiranda or Book of Wonders, states that the waters of the Reatean Marshes were remarkable for hardening the hoofs of horses. Eudicus reports that in Thessaly there were two springs, one named Geron, and that if sheep drank of the waters of this spring, they were turned *black*. The other spring was named *Melas*, and if black sheep drank of that spring, they were turned white ; and that if the same sheep drank of both springs, they became speckled.

Theophrastus also reports that both cattle and sheep that drank of the River Crathis, in Lower Italy, were made white and delicate, whereas the water of the Sybyris gave them a black hue ; and moreover, the same difference was noted among the inhabitants of that country. In Macedonia those that would have white cattle, drove them to drink at the Aliacon, and those that wished for brown or black cattle, drove them to the River Axius ; and further, that those two waters affect even the color of the vegetables growing on their banks in like manner.

In Bœotia, near the Temple of Trophonius, were two fountains; one that exceedingly helped the memory, while the other caused oblivion. Varro speaks of a river in Cilicia, near Crescum, the drinking of whose waters made people far more witty than before. At Chios was a spring that caused despondency, and another at Zamia, in Africa, that gave a clear, shrill voice. If a man drank of the water of Lake Clitonus, he lost all relish for wine, because (as Theopompus says) it made all drunk that used it.

Polyclitus describes a fountain in Cilicia, whose fluid proved a substitute for oil, and Theophrastus another of like quality in Ethiopia. Lycus reports a similar spring in India, used for lamps, and yet another at Ecbatane, the capital of Media.

In Phrygia, near the town of Celænae, were two springs, one of which is said by Theophrastus to produce laughing, and the other weeping, and that they were so named accordingly.

Ctesias speaks of a Pool in India, in which nothing will swim, but all sinks to the bottom, and Coelius reports the same of leaves that fall into Lake Avernus. But in the Lake Apuscidamus in Africa, the water is so dense that nothing will sink. The same has been reported of the well of Saturn in Media.

Pliny reports a river in Bythinia, by the temple of Bryazus, the drinking of whose waters was sure to detect a perjured person, by creating internal inflammation, and also states that the three sources of the great river Tamaricus in Spain, were endued with the secret virtue to presage and foretell future events. These fountains ceased to flow and became dry at least three times a day, notwithstanding a spring near by flowed without intermission.

If persons visited these fountains and found them flowing, good fortune was supposed to attend them, and on the contrary if found dry, as was especially noted in the visit of Lartius Licinius, Lord Praetor and Lieutenant-General under the Consuls. Indudea, a small river, was said to omit flowing regularly every Sabbath day.

Ctesias reports a river in Armenia abounding with fishes, but if any person ate of those fishes they died very soon afterward. The same was said to happen to all who ate of the fishes of the extreme head waters of the Danube. The same was said surely to happen to all who ate of the fishes in the Pool of the Nymphs in Lydia.

Pliny, in his Natural History, relates that in Arcadia near to the River Peneus, a water floweth out of the rocks called Styx, so corrosive and pungent that it would eat its way through all vessels containing it except the hoof of a mule. Theophrastus states that fishes lived in the water of the Styx, as deadly as the water. Theopompus describes the waters of Thrace called Cropsos, which killed those that drank thereof. Lycus also mentions a fountain among the Leontines, of which if people drank they died within three days.

Near the hill of Soracte (says Varro), there was a boil-ing fountain four feet in diameter: this water was well tasted, but many animals and particularly birds, that drank thereof, died upon the spot. A very cold spring of this description existed at Nouacris in Arcadia.

In the beautiful Vale of Tempe, in Thessaly, was a fearful spring that rapidly consumed brass and iron.

In Macedonia, near the Tomb of Euripides the Poet, two rivers flowed together. The one most wholesome to drink, the other noisome and deadly. Anciently there were found cold petrifying waters in Troas, and hot petrifying springs in Delium Eubœa. At Eurymenæ in Thessaly, was a well that petrified all chaplets and gar-lands thrown into it. (The same is seen at the present day in the cave at Matlock in Derbyshire).

At Colossee in Phrygia, was a river into which the in-habitants put unburned bricks and tiles to make them hard instead of burning them. In the famous caves of Corycia, the drops of water percolating through the roof congealed into stalactites like icicles. There was a won-derful exhibition of this nature at Meza in Macedonia, where gigantic stal..ctites were suspended from the vaulted roofs of caverns. At the fountain of Juno in Mesopotamia, the water was said to have a very agreea-ble odor, and to retain its pleasant odor some time after it was taken from the spring.

The celebrated " Flumen Oblivionis" or river of for-getfulness—the Lethe of the ancients, flowed in the channel of the river Limea (now called Lima), in the

western part of Spain.   It obtained the name of Lethe
because a party of Celts on a warlike expedition, by
drinking of its waters wandered away, lost their com-
mander, and even *forgot* the object of their expedition.
The legend was afterward so generally believed, that
Brutus Gallaicus with great difficulty led his army over
this water when he invaded Gallacia, B. C. 136.

From this and like circumstances relating to the trib-
utary of the Meander in Ionia, and the stream identified
with the gardens of the Hesperides sprung the Lethean
fables, in the same manner that Lucian founded his dia-
logues of the dead on the river Styx, after Antipater at-
tempted to poison Alexander with its waters.

But of all fountains on record, none was considered so
extraordinary and wonderful as the Fons Solis or Foun-
tain of the Sun, described by Strabo, Herodotus and
Diod Sic, and situated in a beautiful grove under the
walls of the Temple of Jupiter Ammon in the Great
Lybian Desert.   It was called *"Oraculum Hammonis,"*
twelve days from Cairo, and one hundred and sixty miles
from the Mediterranean inland.   During the middle ages
it was called *Santariah*, and now by the Arabs, Siwah.

The plain or valley surrounding this remarkable spring
is described as fifteen miles long, twelve broad, and two
hundred feet higher than the valley of the Nile, sur-
rounded with a circle of limestone hills so as effectually
to protect from the shifting sands of the desert.

Here numerous springs broke out both fresh and
saline, the fertility surpassed description, and the whole

Oasis was literally a green island as it were, deluged with vegetation, and yet in an ocean of sand. The latitude is twenty-nine degrees north, so that the sun in summer was nearly vertical.

The peculiarity of the water in the fountain was that it was moderately warm at sunrise and gradually grew colder till noon, when it was of icy coldness. Then the temperature began to rise and went on increasing till midnight, when it was boiling hot. Afterwards the heat moderated so that at sunrise it was warm as before.

The mystery of this fountain, so wonderful and inexplicable to the ancients, is easily solved by the aid of geological investigation and the principles of hydrostatics. The Oasis, as we have before said, was surrounded by limestone hills, which in all probability, as usual contained numerous subterranean caverns. These caves would give rise to intermitting or syphon springs similar to those now found in the limestone valleys of Virginia and Kentucky. The cave in the hillside would be filled slowly by innumerable capillary tubes, set together in the form of a strainer, while when full its body of water would be discharged through one channel or opening in half the time required for filling it. Here then were two syphon springs intermitting alternately, one hot, the other cold, both discharging their waters from the same outlet on the surface. At noon the cold one alone flowed, while the hot one was filling, while at midnight the hot one alone flowed, and the cold cask or cavern was being filled ; in the intermediate time their waters

were commingled, and the temperature graduated accord-
ingly.   !

It is not uncommon for both cold and hot springs to
rise out of the ground in juxtaposition. The hot springs
of Virginia rise out of limestone rock, and while you
may scald one hand in the hottest of these springs, you
may hold the other at the same time in a spring painfully
cold. Now if these springs intermitted alternately, as
many springs do in limestone districts by bringing them
into one channel, the same effect would be produced at
the hot springs in Virginia as in the Oasis of the Lybian
Desert.

We will now leave the mystic fountains of the ancients
with their retinue of nymphs and sybils, in order to de-
scribe those of more modern date, which, notwithstand-
ing the *light* of science and civilization, are still clothed
with the darkness of ignorance and blind supersti-
tion.

! There are at this time in the western district of Eng-
land, a large number of wells and springs, and at least
ten or twelve in Wales, all of which are supposed to pos-
sess extraordinary virtues. These are identified with as
many wonderful saints, and their marvellous effects are
still conspicuous in working miracles, healing diseases,
as well as conferring domestic authority upon husband
or wife, who shall first drink of their waters after the
solemnization of marriage.

At the well of St. Enny in Cornwall, women assemble
on Holy Thursday, and throw pins into the clear water,

observing how the heads and points lay, for thereby in their belief, their future fortune is determined.

On other particular days, people collect at St. Madern's well near Penzance, and stamp upon the ground, believing their fate to be determined by the bubbles that rise in consequence.

Bishop Hall, in his "Mysteries of Godliness," has descanted largely on the virtues of this well, and the popular belief in its efficacy has by no means ceased, for here cripples still are cured by its oracular waters, but in all cases according to the measure of faith in the invalid.

Another spring or well in the same neighborhood is dedicated to St. Keyne, near to a church of the same patron saint.

This well not only possesses wonderful healing properties, but is sure to give undisputed authority to husband or wife, who first drinks of it after being married at St. Keyne's Church. Carew in his Poem says of this well:

> " The quality that man or wife,
>   Whose chance or choice attains
>   First of this sacred stream to drink,
>   Thereby the mastery gains."

Of late years the young brides have learned to outwit their husbands by carrying a bottle of the water to the church, so as to drink immediately at the conclusion of the ceremony.

If from Cornwall now we proceed to Wales, we shall find in the southern part of the Isle of Barri, off Cardiff a beautiful clear spring, where, as at St. Enny in Corn-wall, women assemble on Holy Thursday, and after wash-ing their eyes in the clear water, drop pins into the spring to determine their future good or ill success.

The well of St. Beuno was for a long time noted for curing the rickets and other maladies, but it has of late given place to the still more remarkable well or fountain of St. Winnifred, which is reckoned among the seven wonders of Wales.

This well gushes impetuously from a rock at the foot of a hill, and is covered with a gothic structure of great beauty, said to have been erected by Margaret, mother of Henry VII. By a decree in Chancery it has been thrown open to the public, and Catholics resort to it, be-lieving that it has lost none of its legendary virtues.

A pamphlet published to substantiate the character of this supernatural fountain is entitled "Authentic Docu-ments, relative to the miraculous cure of Winnefred White, of Wolverhampton, at Trefynnon or Holy Well, Flintshire, on 28th June, 1805, with Observations thereon by J. M., etc,, etc."

Two festivals are observed here, one in memory of the martyrdom of St. Winnefred, on the 22d of June, and another for her translation to heaven, on the 3d of No-vember. The water passes through an arch into a square court, where devotees were accustomed to swim as an act of penance.

The origin of the well is quite as miraculous as its effects. Saint Winnefred was the beautiful daughter of

a Welsh nobleman named Thewith, and niece of St.
Bueno. She obtained leave of her father to found a
Church here, and having made a vow of perpetual chasti-
ty, was taken under the especial patronage of *St. Buenc
Caradog*, a young Prince, son of King Alen, admiring her
beauty, went one Sunday morning after her father and
mother had gone to church, to ask her hand in marriage.
Instead of giving him an answer, she runs on the hill-
side for the church: Caradog pursues, and on receiving
from Winnefred a *decided* refusal, was so enraged that he
drew his sword and cut off her head at a blow. As the
story goes, Caradog fell dead on the spot, and was never
seen after. Winnefred's head rolled down the hill to the
altar where the congregation were kneeling, and there
stopping, the fountain immediately gushed up. St.
Beuno caught up her head and joined it to the body,
which immediately reunited, the place of separation be-
ing marked only by a white line around the neck. The
sides of the well were thenceforth covered with a sweet-
scented moss, and the stones at the bottom became
tinctured with her blood. She survived decapitation
fifteen years, and having received a veil from St. Elerius,
to hide the scar upon her neck and protect her beauty
against vulgar gaze, became Abbess of a Monastry in
Derbyshire, and there died.

On her decease the well, of course, became endowed
with many miraculous properties.

With all due deference to Romish tradition (says Rev.
Mr. Nicholson), the sweet scented moss is found to be

nothing more than the Jungermania Asplenoides, well
known in Botany, and the supposed tincture of her blood
on the rocks at the bottom of the Byssus iolithus of Lin-
næus and the Lepraria iolithus of Smith.

The devotees of the saint were formerly very numer-
ous, but of late have somewhat diminished, leaving their
crutches and hand-barrows among the ornaments that
adorn the Gothic roof.

This wonderful spring, of which Horace would say :
" O Fous splendidior vitro," discharges at least eighty-
four hogsheads per minute, never freezes or scarcely
varies in drought or the greatest rains.

Thus we see how wily superstition throws her chains
and fetters around mankind in the use of one of the
simplest elements of life, blinding them to the sight of
heaven and common sense, leading reason into bewilder-
ment, and yet at the same time revealing through the
mists of ignorance the great and important fact that
cleanliness next to godliness is great gain, healing most
of the maladies "life is heir to."

It is the province of Chemistry and Philosophy to
strip off this dark mask of superstition and ignorance,
and to show mankind what this essential element of
water really is. Not mechanically, as in the broad ocean
where it is the handmaid of commerce and the highway
of nations—not in the large rivers where it becomes the
foundation and opulence of cities, uniting mankind in a
great scheme of Providence, conveying from shore to
shore, and interchanging from town to town the produc-

tions of the earth ; but chemically as when it is necessarily and economically regarded as the common food of the vegetable and animal kingdoms, chemically and philosophically as it becomes connected with agriculture and the various mechanic arts, as in its elastic state of steam it propels the fleetest ships, drives the fiery car, and in various ways performs the labor of half the human race. Philosophically, as penetrating the atmosphere and circulating over our heads, it becomes associated with the whole doctrine of ærial and atmospheric phenomena, forming a home and hiding-place for the fierce lightning, assisting largely in painting the beautiful scenery of the sky in the economy of clouds and vapor, yielding alternately its most essential nourishment to man in fertilizing showers and the gentle dews of heaven ; and finally, chemically, as a universal cleanser and purifier, and thereby rendered the most appropriate symbol of the purity of heart and life, without which no man shall see the Lord.

TANNING.

SKINS, when fresh, are soaked eight hours in running water, the dry ones being taken out every day and softened on the leg. Then put in solution made by boiling two parts wood ashes and one of quick lime; then decanting this liquor into a vat and diluting it with a sufficient quantity of water, grating on bottom to keep skins from the ashes. In eight days hair removed, then scraped with round knife, then tied on stick and put in running water to wash off ashes, etc. After three days, taken out and washed on hair side, and hung up to drain, fleshed and trod out with the feet. The smaller skins are now soaked twenty-four hours in a trough, filled with a mixture of fecula canis et aqua thermâ, then taken out, cleansed, rinsed, and macerated for twenty-four hours in bath made of oatmeal and malt, then deposited in tan liquor for three days, then sprinkled over with finely powdered oak bark, and piled up above the grating of the vat, which is filled with equal parts of water and tan liquor. The small ones

remain in this for eight days, the larger, longer. After
this, taken out, rinsed, trod out, fleshed, put back in vat,
after being sprinkled over with tan powder as before.
This repeated four times, last time left in vat four weeks,
then taken out, stretched and dried, and given to the
currier to polish and color.

RED PRODUCED FOR ONE HUNDRED SKINS.

Two pounds and nine ounces of alum is used and
eighteen ounces of red sandal for each large skin, and
nine ounces for each small one. The skins are sewed
. around in small stitches, forming sacks, except a small
opening for the coloring matter. After coloring, var-
nished with birch bark and whale oil, and when nearly
dry, subjected to the grainer or cylinders covered with
wire or spirally grooved ; dried and sprinkled with hemp-
seed oil, and polished on the horse.

Lombardy poplar contains 3.12 per cent. tannin, giv-
ing an odor like that of Russian leather.

The leather made from kid and lamb skins owes its
agreeable odor to the bark of the willow with which it is
tanned.

ROTCH'S PROCESS OF TANNING

Is causing tanning fluid to penetrate one side while
artificial heat causes the water that passes through the
other side to evaporate, increasing the strength of the
tan in the leather, and preparing leather thereby in ten
days, which would otherwise require ten months.

RUSSIAN SKINS,

When ready for tanning, are put in a warm solution of salix cinerea and salix caprea, immersed and worked in it half an hour, repeated twice daily for a week, then fresh decoctions another week, then dried, dyed and oiled with birch, etc.

RUSSIAN LEATHER.

The color of red sandal is probably put on with a brush.

MINERAL TANNING.—*Bordier's Process.*

Digest twenty-two pounds of powdered green copperas with two and a quarter pounds nitric acid, Spe. G. 1333, and three pounds sulph. acid, in large stone jars, heated by steam, repeatedly stirring it (avoiding the red poisonous fumes), until the mixture is cold and pasty. After twenty-four hours, dilute with water q. s., and add freshly prepared hydrated per oxide of iron in excess, and after standing four days, with occasional stirring, is ready for tanning. Per oxide of manganese may be used instead of nitric acid.

Soak the skins in this, properly diluted, three days for thin skins, and eight days for sole leather; sub sulphate of iron is absorbed—sulphuric and nitric acids remain in the mother liquor.

CAVALLIN'S PROCESS.

First macerate the skins in a solution of alum and chrome salt, then in a solution of proto sulphate of iron; reaction and interchange of elements ensue, so that the compound of iron and chrome unite indissolubly with the tissue of the hide to form leather, which is brown, tough, compact, and after much soaking, does not lump under the hammer. The hides must be unhaired by lime, drenched thoroughly, rinsed and hung up to drain; avoid using acids in any way.

Bath.—Dissolve ten pounds bichromate of potash and twenty pounds of alum in 180 pounds of water; immerse for four days, drawing them once every twenty-four hours, allowing them to drain, and rubbing them each time as they are returned to the bath, and keep up the strength of the liquor by new additions, by one of chrome and two of alum.

PROTO SULPH. IRON BATH.

Dissolve ten pounds green copperas in sixty pounds of cold water, suspend the skins so as not to touch each other, and draw them once in twelve hours and return them to the bath sufficiently to complete the tanning. Upper leathers require five to six, Swedish sole eight to ten, and American butts thirteen to nineteen days' immersion in the liquor. The strength must be kept up by additions of copperas throughout the treatment. Lastly, take them out, hang up and drain free from slimy matter; soak thoroughly in running water, so as to wash out all saline matter, and finish in usual manner. Upper leathers made in this way are said to be supple and soft,—is blacked by Mordent sat. solution of alum, with eight parts copperas, and then rubbing over strong decoction of logwood, then oiled and finished in usual manner.

DYE TANNING,

Based on the fact that gelatine, dissolved in a decoction of Brazil, Heath, or Fernambogue or other dye wood, is precipitated as an insoluble compound on the addition of a little chrome salt. First immerse in a solution of alum of four ounces to the gallon, or rather preparatory, immerse in a dye of one gallon of the above dye with four gallons of water; must be frequently stirred, lie in for twelve hours, then hung up till nearly dry, then laid in the strong dye and stirred three or four times a day, till dyed through. Then hung up to drain before putting in the chrome bath of ten pounds bichromate of potash to 180 gallons of water for twenty-four hours, drawing them and allowing to drop three or four times, then hung up, drained, then soaked three times in running water for twenty-four hours.

The Bath must be frequently refreshed by additions of chrome salt. Lastly, put in the drying room, stretched smooth, blacked and oiled. Sole leather needs no stirring.

CREATION.

ALMIGHTY GOD, Jehovah, He
First willed and said " Let waters be."
Almighty God, the Infinite,
Then willed and said " Let there be Light."
Enkindled flames preceding years
Rolled into suns and moons and spheres !
Matter thus formed at his command
Receives its motion from His hand.
Matter thus formed from nought before *
Receives its impress evermore.
Throughout the vast extended space
New suns are formed and fixed in place,
Till systems numerous as the sand
Move all harmonious by His hand.
Galaxies vast in depth and height,
Baptised afresh in new-born light,

---

* If God did not create matter from nothing, except his own wil', then something
besides God has existed from Eternity, or otherwise two Eternals—an absurdity.

Are planted in the depth afar
With blazing gems in every star!
While ages that on ages rolled,
In numbers more than can be told.
More clusters into being came
Than I am able here to name,
Or time allow me to rehearse,
Upbuilding God's vast universe.

CREATIONS ON THE FIRST DAY OF THE SOLAR SYSTEM.

On the bright shore of Milky-way
Bursts forth our Sun, blest orb of day!
And circling planets round him shine
Obedient to the hand Divine.
Hence as an offshoot from the Sun
Earth's revolution is begun,
But cloudy vapors soon divide,
And Earth from Sun awhile do hide,
Till day and night opposed appear,
And Day the First begins the Year.

CREATIONS ON THE SECOND DAY OF OUR SOLAR SYSTEM.

The Waters flow on every side
Till God the waters does divide,
When beauty to our World is lent,
Encompassed by the Firmament,
To let bright sunbeams bear the sway
And thus complete the Second Day!

CREATIONS ON THE THIRD DAY OF OUR SOLAR SYSTEM.

The mountains now their heads do rear
And sunny plains at length appear,

The clouds are scattered by the breeze,
And waters gather into seas ;
The Grass now clothes the verdant plain,
Trees, flowers, and fruits and waving grain—
Enchantingly the Earth doth sing
The Third Day's labor of her King.

CREATIONS ON THE FOURTH DAY OF THE SOLAR SYSTEM.

As Time must have its destined sway
And place assigned in the Fourth Day,
Sun, Moon, and Stars are called to aid,
And thus the base of ages laid
For our Terrestial Sphere to claim
Its own duration and its name.

CREATIONS ON THE FIFTH DAY OF OUR SOLAR SYSTEM.

The Waters now awake to life
And Fishes swarm in playful strife,
Birds crowd the air with rapid wing,
As from the deep huge monsters spring ;
The Eagle plumes and soars away
As twilight shuts the Fifth long Day.

CREATIONS ON THE SIXTH DAY OF OUR SOLAR SYSTEM.

The Land is now electrified,
And creatures move on every side ;
Of Beasts, all sorts, and creeping things—
A wondrous herd Sixth Morning brings
Forth on Earth their powers to try,
Both to increase and multiply.

CREATION OF MAN.

Thus far Creation is confined
To various structures without mind ;
But now God's Spirit breathes from heaven,
And life, immortal life, is given.
A thrill through all creation ran—
Behold ! the wondrous Being—Man !
In God's own image, upright made
Of all on earth the destined head,
With mind and reason, far above
The animals that round him move.
But man alone unfinished is—
Some one to share his sympathies—
An " help meet " needs to make him whole
And fill the measure of his soul.
He lies him down in sleep to rest,
Most deeply yearning to be blest :
Again God's Spirit breathes from heaven—
From his own breast is Woman given.
Both now are one in heart and soul ;
Both are but parts of one great whole ;
Each made to serve for other's good,
Never to differ if they would ;
In virgin sweetness loving, she
Yields unto man her destiny—
The last best gift to man, to be
In innocence and purity—
Creation's climax—chief of all
Organic forms on earthly ball.
The Sixth day's labor, now complete,
The Morning Stars their songs repeat ;

Unnumbered worlds their anthems raise
To herald their Creator's praise !

THE SEVENTH DAY.

The Seventh Day morning now appears,
Like the preceding days or years,
Consistent with those gone before,
In time the same—no less, no more.
Jehovah lays his work aside
And views the starry heavens spread wide.
Unnumbered worlds their songs employ—
Unnumbered beings filled with joy—
His vast domain is yet untrod ;
O what a vision for a God !
This Seventh Day's most divinely blest—
Jehovah's day for holy rest.
Thrice holy hence its hours let be,
In worship pure and charity,
Till all Seventh days, to man thus given,
Prepares his soul to enter heaven.

GEOLOGICAL INFIDELITY IN GOD'S RECORD OF CREATION.

But men there are who rise and say
God's eve and morning mean *not* day,
But something else they cannot tell,
And thus uphold the Infidel.
How low their views of God must be,
Omnipotence in Deity !

How little know the powers that ply
Through ocean, earth, the air, the sky ;
What elements convened will do,
Instanter working wonders new !
Could they but stand aside and see
The handy work of Deity—
Magnetic streams the mountains form,
Galvanic piles their work perform,
Crystallic forces, early, late,
All earth at once precipitate ;   \
The acids seize the alkalies
And bubbling effervescence rise ;
The mingling gasses rapidly
Fill the vast ocean to the sky,
To cool electric streams of fire—
How would they wonder, how admire !
Would they their calculation try
And find how races multiply,
By doubling each quintuple year
A strange result would then appear
Of shells more numerous than the sand
On Ocean's shore, or leaves on land :
E'en in the years before the flood,
By figures sure well understood,
In twenty years now let us see
If man could not well doubled be.
In sixteen hundred, then 'tis clear,
A billion souls on earth appear
Before the flood had swept away
Said billion from the light of day.

Let us again our Bible read
And to its word give special heed ,
On this quotation thought employ,
· "Lo ! Man with earth will I destroy."

—GEN. vi. 13.

THE DELUGE.

What overturnings must have been
In Earth's destruction for Man's sin !
The mountains washed quite to their base,
And Ocean's bed much changed in place,
Volcanoes opening many rents
And Earthquakes lifting Continents !
Yet these men say, "Improbable,
Such changes are too notable ;
We cannot see how coal was made
In such short time as Moses said,
Or great fish-lizards fill the seas
Instead of whales in times like these,
Or big bone mammals traverse earth
Posterior to old Adam's birth.
We do believe that Nature tells
Of countless ages in the shells,
Of ocean's bed, and inland bogs,
Where sported once huge polywogs ;
And goblins danced for ages more
Ere man appeared upon the shore.
Long time it took for trees to grow,
Sufficient for the coal you know ;
Then must they sink beneath the tide—
Strange sorts of fishes o'er them ride ;

And some of them yet caught within,
For now behold their scales are seen.
Then sands wash on to form the stone,
Used now for building hard as bone.
As fermentation slow goes on,
Long time it takes to form carbon.
The seam then comes above the surf—
Is strewed with seeds and green with turf;
Till trees again the whole o'erspreads,
When down they go to form new beds.
All this before a man was seen
To pluck the fruit in Eden green.
Now by the single rule of three,
We trace each coal-bed's history.
If one alone such time requires,
The whole no less than myriad years:
But then the cooling we forgot,
Our molten world, at first so hot;
As lava cools so slow, we say,
Millions of years make just one day.
The icebergs then, we have been told,
For ages chained the earth in cold—
And hence it is well understood
That afterwards there was a flood !
What ages then to form the sand,
Composing rocks in New Holland,
Thousands of feet in thickness laid,
As seen from sea the shoreland head.
Now all these ages, side by side,
With numbers more not multiplied,

Shut up in space six thousand years—
What monstrous folly it appears !
The Bible Record, thus you see,
Is not considered *true to be.*"
Had these men seen a chicken hatch
In some lone place spread o'er with thatch,
They would conclude quite otherwise,
With ample proof before their eyes.
From one cold egg all this is done—
Blood warmed for days just twenty-one.
What has produced the change they see ?
Ah ! the galvanic battery !
With this addition, to be sure,
The simple rise of temperature.
How great the change ! how short the time !
From albumen, the yolk, the lime.
Thus much effected by the hen,
In countless years what might be seen !
Just fourteen elements in all
Mature the chick within the ball.
Or should they trial make with clay,
Well stirred with water we would say,
Let stream galvanic through it run,
Twelve months at least the work is done :
'Tis slate upright, without dissent,
As proved by Hunt's experiment.
Should they another trial make
With sediment from some mud lake ?
Let stream magnetic flow again,
Two kinds of rock would they obtain—

Amorphous one, and trap beside,
As seen in hills that plains divide.
If twelve months' time doth this effect
On currents vast, let us reflect.

FORMATION OF COAL.

And now the Coal-beds, how are they
Formed from vast forests swept away?
By river tides, like Amazon,
Into the seas with sands upon
Them, till as dough from baken bread
Yeast fermentations through them spread!
With increased heat as new freights come,
When ash becomes potassium—
Carbonic acid present then
At once gives up its oxygen,
And leaves the carbon to explain
Each kind of wood, the very grain,
Just like the writing on a note
When burnt to ash, away to float.
The sifting action of the sea
Gathers the sand one family ;
Also the iron, clay, and lime,
For heat to harden in short time,
And rise to light, and bloom as Eden,
As rises now the coast of Sweden.

GREAT SANDSTONE FORMATION OF AUSTRALIA.

At last remain the banks of sand,
Formed into stone in New Holland,

(On this vast rock great pains are spent
To found *the strongest* argument ;)
In height three thousand feet or more,
Extending far the island o'er.
In explanation of this fact
Observe volcanoes how they act,
Outpouring lava in a tide
Into the ocean far and wide,—
Soon as saltwater meets the stream
We then behold the power of steam,
Reducing it at once to * sand,
Upfilling vallies—forming land.
The saline steam serves a cement
In building this new continent ;
Northward and East Australia
Volcanoes countless wildly play,

---

* The great eruptions, a lava falling into the sea in the Sandwich Islands, particularly that of the Volcano Kilauea, June 1st, 1840, described by Rev. Mr. Cown, in Missionary Herald, Vol. 37, page 283. The following is an extract from Rev. Titus Cown's letter: "Imagine to yourself a river of fused minerals of the breadth and depth of Niagara, and of a deep gory-red falling in one emblazoned sheet, one raging torrent into the ocean ! The scene as described by eye-witnesses was terribly sublime. Two mighty agencies in collision. Two antagonistic and gigantic forces in contact and producing effects inconceivably grand ! The atmosphere in all directions was filled with ashes, spray, gases, etc., while the burning lava as it fell into the water was shivered into millions of minute particles, and being thrown back into the air, fell in showers of sand on all the surrounding country. The coast was extended far into the sea for a quarter of a mile, and a pretty sand beach formed. Three hills of scoria and sand were also formed in the sea, the lowest about two hundred feet, and the highest about three hundred feet. For three weeks this terrific river discharged itself into the sea with little abatement. Multitudes of fishes were killed and the waters of the ocean were heated for twenty miles along the coast."

Evolving molten streams of fire
From 'neath the sea and mountains higher.
These streams converted into sand,
What else to form but New Holland?—
To rise and shine like other lands,
Though mostly formed of arid sands.

CONCLUSION.

Now in conclusion we would say
A few more words on Sabbath-day,
To those who think the seventh *not* **past,**
And countless ages yet to last.
Their logic strange, yet quite as good
As that they use ere came the "*Flood.*"
If the seventh day *is yet* to last—
Who can *remember* what's *not past ?*

Let us in adoration fall
Before Jehovah, Lord of all,
Nor vex ourselves too much about
His wondrous ways, "past finding out."
How long or short the time may be,
When measured by eternity !
Sufficient for us all to know
That to the Judgment we must go,
Reap the reward of actions here
In worlds unknown beyond our sphere,
Where God's *Great Laws* illumined bright,
Will endless shine in clearest light.

MOSES OXYGEN

EDINBURGH, May 31, 1866.

THE GOLDEN CALF:

OR THE

ALMIGHTY DOLLAR.

FREEDOM had fled from Earth with bitter tears,
Finding no spot which she could claim as hers :—
Now hail'd by men, with greetings of pure joy,
And now rejected as a worthless toy,
Now worship'd and rever'd by all mankind,
Now torn from hearts where she was late enshrin'd,
She saw that those, who by her care she'd bless
With all things that insure man's happiness,
Turn'd from her shrine of pure simplicity,
Lur'd by the golden pomp of tyranny ;
And gave up all most dear for man to own,
To bend before a sceptre and a throne.

Hopeless, she fled, in sad despondency,
And wept to think man never would be free.
But when a New World from the ocean rose,
Among its wilds a rugged home she chose :
On her bright mission coming yet once more,
Beaming with hope, she lit upon our shore,
Resolv'd to strive to build, across the sea,
A lasting monument to Liberty,
And show the world a truth of high intent—
That men are equal to self-government.
See the result—though but of recent birth,
We stand among the greatest pow'rs of earth :
From thirteen States despised, and weak, and poor,
Our empire reaches, now, to either shore ;
And as it, thus, with giant pow'r expands,
The railroad links it with its iron bands,
While fleets of steamboats throng our inland seas,
And Commerce bends her sails to ev'ry breeze ;
In the Far West, whole forests swept away,
Cities arise where they stood yesterday,
And Agriculture, with her fruitful hand,
Sows plenty broadcast o'er our favor'd land ;
While Education opens unto all
The old log field-school, or the college hall.

And now the Old World gazes in surprise,
To mark our greatness, and our sudden rise ;
And tyrants, and decay'd nobility,
Fear that their serfs, who our example see,
May turn upon the foot that's crush'd so long,
And by one effort strike down hoary wrong.

But—sad reflection—nations once were free,
As great, and far more powerful than we,
Who now are fallen, most corrupt, and base,
Degraded, and a stigma on their race ;
Potent no more, except in what depraves,
They move upon the earth as crawling slaves.
See Rome, now impotent and fall'n, hurl'd
From her proud place as Mistress of the World ;
Gone all her pow'r, and gone her dauntless pride,
And strength which, singly, all the world defied ;
Gone her proud monuments, her temples gone,
Her forum but a shapeless mass of stone ;
Her navy gone, her boasted army is
Replac'd by regiments of hireling Swiss ;
Her name, that once could haughtiest monarchs tame,
Becomes a by-word for disgrace and shame.
Yet once the meanest of that grov'ling herd,
The while a haughty pride his bosom stirr'd,
Had stood defiant, e'en to kings, to claim
That homage due unto a Roman's name.

Then let us seek to trace th' unvarying cause
Which rules all nations with unerring laws ;
And, found, let us endeavor to avoid
That one great vice by which they're all destroy'd,
For all the experience of the past will teach,
That else we their degraded state must reach.
'Tis love of gold, the parent vice of all
Those other vices which weak man enthrall ;
For wealth, well used, by Providence design'd
To make a nation glorious and refin'd,

Is far too apt to ruin, and deprave,
Degrade the good, and enervate the brave.
The rich, indulging in each vile excess,
Mistake debauchery for happiness,
And by base revel, and the low debauch,
Fan into flame their country's fun'ral torch.
The poor, who thus their bad example view,
Demoralized, forget the instincts true
Of man to good, and, imitating them,
Lose all the noble attributes of men,
Till, plung'd in an excess of luxury,
Corruption, vice, and crime, at last we see
The long-doom'd nation totter to its fall,
And melancholy ruin whelming all.

Thus it has ever been, will ever be,
Like the fatal fruit of the dead lotos-tree,
Which floats its vot'ries on delicious dreams,
And pours enchanting thoughts, in plenteous streams,
Through the enraptured brain, and, for the time,
Brings visions bright, and glorious, and sublime,
But leads the man, through pleasures, most intense,
Unto a dark and awful impotence.

Shall we then make the golden calf divine,
And place his statue in a holy shrine?
Shall we begin to bend to, and adore,
An idol that is fatal evermore?
And shall we this religion drear adopt,
That's ever found so false and so corrupt?

Sad truth we have—so pleasing are its rites,
Each day brings in new crowds of proselytes,
The worship now begun—we'll place us nigh,
And see each fervent neophyte pass by.

Far be't from me to sneer at those whose place
Would mark them as the teachers of their race,
Who, if sincere, like their great Master, should
Go about.ever seeking to do good :
Here to give comfort, there to chide, or warn
The sinner's feet from paths that lead to harm ;
To tend the sick, console some racking grief,
Or lead the doubter on to firm belief ;
Thrice happy lot, to them also 't is given,
To turn the thoughts of criminals to heav'n,—
Little by little to inculcate good,
And lead these from a life of hardihood,
To learn the error of their ways, and trust
A God that's always merciful and just,
While Faith's blest light upon their bosoms pours,
And substitutes repentance for remorse.
A life like this is truly good and pure,
And, if sincere in't, none could wish for more ;
And though, undoubtedly, some faithful few
Are conscientious in whate'er they do,
Yet many a clergyman, I'm much afraid,
Adopts his calling as he would a trade,
And while he'd scorn to be a humble teacher,
Strives to become a fashionable preacher ;
As if he'd suffer beneath heaven's frown,
Unless he held forth in a church up town.

He tends no sick, he comforts no distress'd,
He gives no aching bosom balmy rest,
He never enters at a humble door,
And ministers unto the suff'ring poor ;
And if he would, how should he have the art,
Lacking two things—sincerity and heart ?
No, once a week, in drawling tones, he pours
Upon a yawning audience a discourse.
His tidy kids are daintily drawn on,
And pure as innocence his spotless lawn.
He waves his kerchief, edged with richest lace,
And lengthens piously his rev'rend face.
He speaks of angel choirs,—his thoughts are far
Among the gems of last night's opera ;
Of heav'nly joys, which no one values less,
And looks admiringly at each new dress ;
Tells us of holy truths to which he's careless,
And looks with venal eye upon some heiress ;
And when the blessing's given, and he's through,
Hastens to Smith's, to dine with a choice few ;
Or of petitions, mayhap, signs a score
'Gainst slavery, which he thinks is a sore
Blot on our nation, and against th' intent
Of the Constitution ; but ne'er gives a cent
To help a freedman, or to buy a slave.
Oh no, he gives his all, the surpliced knave,
In that cheap substitute for charity
Which mock philanthropists call sympathy.
In a few years he tires of the routine,
And wishes, good man, for a change of scene.
When, practising a sort of pious fraud,

He gets bronchitis, and is sent abroad.
Such men too oft—oh, shame unto our kind !—
Among us, in this golden age, we find :
They lead the way where all the others follow,
And worship only the Almighty Dollar.

Then after him behold the sage M. D.,
A weighty man in the community ;
He's your best friend, ador'd too by your wife,
And ushers all your children into life.
In sombre black he drives 'round in a gig,
Takes snuff, chews rhubard, and he wears a wig.
Whene'er a patient he is call'd to see,
Our Esculapius talks most learnedly ;
A poultice he a cataplasm will call,
Bleeding depletion, and, at times, lets fall
A monster word like this one " diarrhetic,"
Which means the opposite to, an emetic.
He hems, and haws, and asks your tongue to see,
And then in Latin writes his recipe ;
And when at fault, puts always " quantum suff.,"
Which in plain English only means enough.
He's a philanthropist—a constant strife
He wages 'gainst the various ills of life ;
When in his presence, hint but at a pain,
And you will try to 'scape his clutch in vain.
He feels your pulse, then questions you quite close,
Inspects your tongue, and orders you a dose ;
And when, at last, you're really made unwell,
He puts a muffle on your front-door bell,

From your abode proscribes your dearest friends,
And hired nurses of his own he sends.
And, after things have gone awhile this way,
He calls upon you four times ev'ry day ;
Ne'er say " I'm better," and ne'er ask " why is it ?"
The Doctor's always paid so much a visit.
You are, my friend—you'll pardon me, I beg—
The goose who lays, for him, the golden egg,
And he's not fool enough, like him of old,
To put an end to that which brings him gold.
Yet he, at length, when forc'd by decency,
Permits you, first, a friend or two to see,
Then lets you rise, a moment, from your bed,
And to your window has you gently led ;
And, when you've this a week or so endur'd,
He then pronounces you completely cur'd,
And sends you in—thank God, the thing's no worse—
A bill, requiring a strong, healthy purse.

Next comes a bustling, busy little man,
Whose restless eyes seek ev'rything to scan.
His pale, thin lips, wreath'd in a constant smile,
Mark him a man of strategy and wile ;
One who has not a sole redeeming trait,
And whom all men should justly execrate :—
He is a man expert in all that's evil,
A Lawyer, and first cousin to the devil ;
A great peace-maker, who, as it appears,
Always pulls folks together by the ears ;
One who has done far more in his life
Towards keeping up fell rancor, and stern strife,

Among the human family, than all
Men of all other kinds since Adam's fall.
He loves to see relations, dearest, learn
To hate each other, let their bosoms burn
With every passion that is base and ill,
Striving, for gold, to break a parent's will.
But most he loves to hunt out an old flaw,
Which proves some title-deed not worth a straw;
Instant he seeks you, and says, Sir, this land
Is yours, if you a little suit can stand;
Explains it all, and makes the thing quite clear,
And you a very injur'd man appear.
While he, one of that philanthropic brood
Of hell's own hatching, seeks naught but your good.
And if, by chance, you to a suit agree,
Before you know it you're in Chancery,
And, well in Chancery, the Lord knows when
You'll live to get well out of it again;
Year after year the thing drags slowly on,
Until at length 'tis over, and you've won.;
And when, at last, you've gotten safely through 't,
He brings a bill in longer than the suit;
He never acts from feelings pure and kind.
But like his goddess, Justice, is quite blind;
Holds out his hand, takes all that he can get,
And counts all fish that come into his net.
Expert in all th' expedients of fraud,
He sets at naught, not man's laws, those of God,
No Christian motives prompt him e'er to lend
His services the suff'ring to befriend.
The wrong'd and cheated are to him as naught,

Provided his opinion is not bought ;
The weak may bend beneath oppression's heel,
Gold is the only touch-stone he can feel :—
Soulless, like corporations, he will act
For either side, and with the nicest tact,
And do the dirtiest things for a good fee,
Provided he can do them legally.

The next man, see, his face all thin with care,
His brow is furrow'd, and all white his hair ;
A merchant, with his coffers running o'er,
Day by day striving to increase his store ;
His ships, deep-laden, plunge through ev'ry sea,
And wealth pours in upon him plenteously.
Yet, as he works assiduous for gain,
Full many blots his flexile conscience stain.
He holds to his word with scruple most intense,
But wrongs at any time his moral sense ;
His boasted honor is a show most hollow,
Which he has sacrificed for many a dollar :
When selling so low that he can but lose,
He's gaining profits that would shock the Jews.
His maxim is his store to increase,
Seem honest, and the unsuspecting fleece ;
If he e'er give a sum in charity,
The thing is done for show, and publicly ;
He gives it thus, because he feels quite sure
That, in the end, he'll gain by it much more,
As actors, now and then to make a hit,
Perform for some asylum's benefit :—

Among the congregation he appears,
One of the calf's most ardent worshipers.

He whom all eyes with such mark'd rev'rence follow,
Is, so to speak, friend, an incarnate dollar
A golden Mars, waging perpetual war
In the stock market, as a bull or bear ;
Or haply owns a bank, not worth a fiddle,
Deep in the bottom, or far in the middle
Of some imaginary lake, with all
Sorts of imaginary capital ;
And when our broker a round sum has made,
You find some day your friend the " wild cat's" dead,
Or your " white pigeon" flown.   A serious joke—
Your broker and his fancy bank are broke,
Or else he issues spurious bonds for stocks,
Or, with a wire, picks his own strong box.
Our quondam bull no more his horn'd head tosses,
But then retires to live upon his losses,
And takes his place (earn'd—oh most worthily—)
As high-priest of the gold divinity.

Behold an editor—see what his tone,
Who rules a reading public, like our own ;
Who, as he works for good, or its reverse,
Becomes a nation's blessing or its curse.
What is his tone ?   He changes hour by hour,
Striving to gain the patronage of pow'r ;
And tries to sway the public by his views,
For his own good this moral force to use.

Hear him the course of factionists lamenting,
Working, the while, to get the public printing
See how, when foil'd in his selfish aims,
His unbias'd sheet th' administration blames ;
Like him who, outraged, shifted his position,
When told he couldn't get a foreign mission.
Yet they have pow'r ; they know it, and they use it—
Unhappily, too often they abuse it ;
This side or that they will denounce, or praise,
According as the rival bidder pays.
Their country's good these patriots ne'er consider,
They always write for him who's highest bidder :—
They're like the rest—they worship that same gold,
And can, at any time, be bought or sold.

Time was when our fair country hail'd, with pride,
The patriot band who rallied to her side ;
No sordid motives their pure breasts imbued,
Who thought of nothing but their country's good ;
No dream of pay or place e'er cross'd their mind,
But, rather, ease or wealth each one resign'd,
And bravely fought, through times of deepest gloom,
For those yet lying in the Future's womb.
Our rights attack'd—the dread alarm is giv'n,
And echoed by the arching vault of heav'n ;
Each infant colony takes up the cry,
And stern men arm to conquer or to die ;
Each noble patriot feels his cause is strong—
'Tis mighty Right contending against Wrong.
Well may each vein with strong emotion thrill,
And honest pride our heaving bosoms fill,

As we behold this firm devoted band
Fight for the freedom of their native land.
Now, campless, bivouacking cheerfully
Among the noxious swamps of the Pedee ;
And now, half naked, leaving, as they go,
Their bloody tracks on Valley Forge's snow ;
And when they've won proud Saratoga's field,
And forc'd, at Yorktown, our stern foe to yield,
Not yet their labors over, nor their care,
The Senate calls them to new duties there ;
And their great aim, throughout the long debate,
To make the people prosperous and great.
Far other now—the Patriots all are dead—
We have the politician in their stead :
A brood of vultures, which around us rise,
Ready to pounce upon each carrion prize.
These men are in the market, and the cry,
"Patriots for plunder, come, who'll buy—who'll
   buy ?"
What care they for the country?   What care they
For those whose votes they canvass'd yesterday ?
Now for economy—it has a charm—
Now vote each lazy vagabond a farm ;
Now fillibusters, and all annexation,
Now it would be destruction to the nation ;
Now they swear ev'ry foreigner 's a rogue,
And now they "love the sound of the dear brogue ;"
To-day Free-soilers, the next Union men,
The next day for the woolly-heads again ;
Now for the highest tariffs, now for small,
For or against just anything at all :—

Vile demagogues, who care not what they say,
Or how they act, provided it will pay.
Selfish, unprincipled, most vile and base,
They'd barter off their souls for pay and place ;
Shame they have none, and honor is a word
The have forgotten ever to have heard.
They worship naught but principle, we're told—
Another name for our same calf of gold.

Who that poor youth whose dress and mien proclaim
One made his sex to burlesque and to shame ?
But just eighteen, a man he apes to be,
Though lacking all to make one worthily ;
Just heart enough to send blood through his veins,
And tongue enough to show his want of brains ;
Man in his vices he can imitate,
Not in one virtue that does palliate ;
His day is spent round stables and 'mong grooms,
Or swallowing brandy in low drinking-rooms ;
At night he to some hell will staggering go,
And lose his father's money at faro ;
Or, in some fashionable brothel, mends
His mind and morals 'mong his female friends.
Nothing that's sensible for him—oh no—
Our brainless man conceives that it's too "slow."
If you e'er ask him how his time is past,
He smiles, and tells you New York 's dev'lish fast ;
Says he has been " out driving on the road,"
Or " in a rum-shop taking on a load ;"
He sups at Claremont with a crowd to-night,
Where doubtless they'll get beautifully "tight ;"

Or mayhap he affects the old roué
And yawns and grumbles, and says he's blasé ;
Has cut the theatres, and parties, too,
And wishes he could get up something new.
But our American taste is very low—
And as for living—why, we don't know how.
He thinks it's dev'lish hard—what do you think?
He feels quite dry—suppose you take a drink.
Look at him—yes, you justly may say faugh—
He is that thing styled "Young America :"
A thing more apt to make you sigh than laugh—
A beast begotten by the Golden Calf.

Behold the two last draw up at the door—
Each one, you see, arrived in coach and four.
Tompkins and Smith, two of the upper-ten,
Who're made by this calf-worship among men.
For upper-tendom—I don't mean to shock it—
Measures a man, friend, by his depth of pocket.
Smith has a large palatial residence,
Furnish'd and built regardless of expense.
Enter and look—what man could wish for more?
There's nothing wanting money 'll buy, I'm sure.
He has *bois de rose*, and *buhl*, and *marquetrie*,
His carpets *Aubusson tapisserie*.
Objets de virtu priceless, rich, and rare,
And our best sculptors' handiwork, are there ;
And pictures, too—although it seems he aims,
In them, at nothing but the richest frames ;
Wheel'd vehicles of all sorts 'neath the sun—

Berline, calèche, coupé, and phaeton ;
His horses are the finest that you'll see,
His servants wear the richest livery :
In fine, he's of the *ton*,—the most elite
Society at Smith's grand balls you meet.
And who is Smith ? To see him, you'd declare
His condescending smile and haughty air
Stamp him a snob—one of the newly great,
Who gain'd his station after his estate :—
Pretension, egotism, and conceit,
Give you our hero's character complete.
Smith was, as all his fellow-townsmen know,
A baker once, who kneaded his own dough ;
Who, when in life he first began to start,
Was not too proud to drive his own bread-cart :
He was industrious, understood his trade,
And, by degrees, a little money made ;
And when, in time, he a small fortune earn'd,
Dough, trough, and shop, and bread-cart, all were
       spurn'd ;
On Wall-street he was early seen, and late;
In town-lots he'd begun to speculate :
He sold and bought, and sold again and bought,
The city grew, lots eagerly were sought ;
Until, at length, things got to such a pitch,
One fine day dawns, and Smith's immensely rich.
And having now made quite enough to dash on,
He thinks he'll enter in the world of fashion.
As the first step, he builds his house up town,
And furnishes it, as already shown
And, as th' aristocratic feeling warms,

He steps down street to buy a coat of arms.
The Herald—for so well this thing does pay,
We have a Herald's office on Broadway—
The Herald asks him, with a solemn phiz,
Which fam'ly of the myriad Smiths is his.
His father was a shoemaker, he knows—
No farther back his genealogy goes.
And therefore, as his questioner knew well,
He answers that he can't exactly tell ;
But other people have them, and he'll pay
As much for one as they can, any day.
The Herald then—" Dear sir, your shield shall be
Made from parts of the prettiest two or three,
That's well enough, and by the way of crest,
We'll take the one that suits your fancy best.'
Now well equipp'd with ev'rything he needs,
To give a splendid ball he next proceeds,
And for the company he sends for Browne,
The sexton of a fancy church up town,
Who always takes around the invitations
To the balls of persons in the " highest stations,"
And by a sequitur which I can't see,
Introduces blackguards in society.
In France nobility has gone so far
For *nouveaux riches*, snobs from America,
As to invite guests to the nabob's ball,
With this proviso, they invited all,
Regarding him as a *restaurateur*
Who furnish'd them with music and good cheer ;
And did it gratis, too, and cheerfully,
Provided he fed aristocracy.

But New-York high-life justly this reverses,
And bends before its man of pews and hearses.
He gives to Smith the names from his own list,
And the next day is with the cards dismiss'd :
Beau-monde turns up its nose awhile, for show,
But finally, concludes that it will go.
The host is vulgar—but he entertains
Uneducated—but a man of means ;
A low upstart, whose talisman's his purse—
My friend, most of them are as bad, or worse.
Besides, we know society's benign
To those who feed it well, and keep good wine :—
Thenceforward Smith holds up his head 'mong men,
And takes his place amid the upper-ten.
When Smith on Fortune's wave began to ride,
Tompkins his trade as a poor tailor plied :
But he, too, wishes in the world to rise,
And, as he works, learns to economize.
He fits quite well, is moderate in charges,
And, with his business, he his shop enlarges ;
Expanding then in views and fortune both,
He turns a merchant, and he deals in cloth.
He imports largely, has " a run of luck,"
And with th' aristocratic feeling's struck.
The first step in his upward path, of course,
Is a fine house, and he builds one perforce ;
But why repeat—like Smith, he calls in Browne,
And fêtes the fashionable part of town.
On Tompkins' house new days begin to dawn,
His hissing goose is, now, a splendid swan.

Although Smith, who preceded him some years,
Has for society's stability great fears ;
Indeed, Smith's family all grow quite savage
At his success, and make hints about cabbage,
While proud Miss Smith, contemptuously, says
She does despise those upstart Tompkinses.

Poor human nature—if these folks must rise,
Why let them, 'tis not they that we despise.
Let them have Crœsus' wealth, or richer be,
We lose not our respectability.
But, once admitted to the place they sought,
Let them remember their position's bought ;
Let them avoid all airs, and all pretension,
Nor always act as if in condescension ;
And above all, when others, good as they,
Rise from a station they held yesterday,
Let them not talk as if they could look, far,
Beyond their own plebeian ancestor.
I'll tell to them a truth the whole world owns,
" Ye dwellers in glass houses, don't throw stones."
No, act with dignity in your new place,
Nor think your origin is a disgrace ;
Try not to hide, nor drag it into view,
Let it alone, the world will do so too ;
Seeking to hide it is a vulgar shame,
To show't a false pride equally to blame.
No—keep the even tenor of your way,
Of others' origin have naught to say ;

Once ris'n, tis contemptible and mean
To sneer at that which you yourselves have been.
You rose through wealth, and let not a purse-pride,
Make others speak of things you'd gladly hide.

It is our country's honor, and its boast
That each man may attain to any post.
Man's mind is free to judge of any fact,
And, as he judges, he is free to act.
Religion, government, whate'er it be,
'Tis still the same, man's mind is always free ;
The people's holy voice decides on all,
Acclaims the statesman, or it dooms his fall ;
And each of those who with his voice's might,
Proclaims his verdict with a freeman's right,
No matter if the humblest of the throng,
Who honor honesty, or punish wrong,
Feels, as he's standing there unknown to Fame,
With nothing his except a freeman's name,
With nothing there to raise him 'bove his kind,
Except the stern will, and the pow'rful mind,—
With not one friend, by place or riches strong,
With but himself to help himself along,—
With conscious pride, feels that great truth sublime,
That he may win a name to last through time ;
That want of birth and wealth gives naught to fear,
Where high or low may run the same career ;
And he, if he have mind and honesty,
The strong resolve, and firm integrity,

May, step by step, rise up and take his place
Among the highest, loftiest of his race ;
May win that post, the proudest man can fill,
The freemen's ruler, by the freemen's will.
Yes, this is so ; but, answer me, how oft
Does worthiest merit bear a man aloft ?
How many men, of intellect and worth,
Are crush'd and kept back, not by want of birth,
But by the want of wealth ?—that cursed god
That rules our nation with a tyrant's rod.
While others, who have not one claim to be
Rais'd from their birth-right of obscurity,
Attain that place which those may vainly crave,
Carried aloft on Fortune's golden wave.
Most sad avowal, yet alas ! too true,
Gold is all pow'rful—gold can all things do.

Yes, glorious gold, 't is thus each day we see
Goodness and truth subservient to thee.
Thou mighty god, near thee all others pale,
Thy power alone it is can never fail.
We bend to thee with superstitious awe,
And humbly greet thy presence from afar.
'Thrice pow'rful Deity, we worship thee
Supreme, oh most august Divinity !
Thee ever honor, to thee give all praise,
And to thy service consecrate our days.
Thou great, benign, serene Omnipotence,
Eagles, half eagles, dollars, dimes and cents.

And still dread awe our throbbing bosom fills,
As we contemplate thee reduced to mills.

How few of those who seek wealth do we see
Who make no sacrifice of honesty ;
How very few of those who wealth inherit
Are ever men of any worth or merit !
The heir, what is he mostly in our day ?
Weak debauchee, or profligate roué ;
His mind is weak and vulgar as his taste,
His moral sense is blunted or debased :
He has the vices, but is lacking quite
The refinement of th' effem'nate Sybarite.
While those who lack wealth, truth most melancholy,
With these vie in extravagance and folly ;
Owing their house-rent, and yet giving balls,
Their butcher, and yet hiring op'ra stalls ;
Preying on him who trusts them, or who lends,
Cheating their tradesmen, and defrauding friends,
Their whole life is a fraud, and a deceit,
Their creed rascality, their aim to cheat ;
Steal a few half-dimes, and the world cries, shame.
Let it be thousands, and you get no blame ;
That is, don't rob a man, that's deadly sin,
And vulgar too—but "make it out of him :"
Go cheat the government, but let it be
A good round sum, and do it legally ;
Then revel on the proceeds of your fraud,
Fear nothing, feast men, and they'll all applaud ;

Defraud an orphan, on your ill-got gains
Give balls, in entertainments spare no pains ;
Go sport you lord-like, build a princely house,
And give a periodical carouse :
And then 't is not the theft that's wrong, you'll see,
But going to the penitentiary.
Men hold the doctrine Spartan boys were taught,
To steal's no sin, but only to be caught.
Riches is what by all is most desir'd,
And who has most of it is most admired.

Who then e'er made th' assertion weak and rash,
And foolish, he "who steals my purse steals trash !"
That great man whom I honor and admire,
Iago, but 'twas when he did desire
To heal the aching pang which gave unrest,
To black Othello's jealous swarthy breast.
'Twas nonsense, and he thus did truth abuse,
Just as good men will often fiction use
To heal some racking pang, and give relief,
Where passion's cur'd by things beyond belief.
But when he spoke words wise and full of truth
To Roderigo his friend, ardent youth,
He said, young man, these words of wisdom nurse,
Above all things, "put money in thy purse."
Yes, lose all honor and all virtue, be
Guilty of ev'ry crime and infamy,
Do each base deed, from which the sicken'd soul
Shrinks back appall'd ; admit not the control

'Of e'en one decent feeling, if you've gold,
Stand safe amid your treasures, and be bold.
Your vice, a dazzling veil is hid behind,
The world to all except your gold is blind
It is the magic that can all bewitch,
YOU'RE SURE TO BE RESPECTABLE IF RICH.

REPORT.

TO THE PRESIDENT AND DIRECTORS

OF THE

VANDERBURG MINING COMPANY.

GENTLEMEN :—

I HAVE, the last month, made a survey of the property belonging to the Vanderburg Mining Company in North Carolina, and herewith send you a map I have prepared of the same, on which the principal veins and important features of the property will be found plotted.

The main tract comprises several estates now consolidated into one. It has an extreme length, north and south, of about one mile and 100 rods, and east and west is nowhere less than 200 rods. It bounds the property of the Phœnix Mining Company on the north and east, and must have upon it the extension of all the veins worked by this Company.

It is about six miles from Concord, in Cubarrus county, to which place the North Carolina Railroad will be in operation next spring.

The surface of the country is elevated ; it is moderately hilly, fertile and well watered. The principal tract is about equally divided between farming and timber land. The growth is mostly oak with groves of small pines. Many large yellow pines are intermixed with the hardwood growth.

The rock formation is greenstone—seldom seen outcropping, but exposed in loose pieces over the surface, and reached below by mining operations. It passes into a highly ferruginous horn-blend rock, with which is associated a little serpentine and epidote. The slate belt of this region lies farther east ; the granite belt is on the west, extending beyond Concord.

A great number of metaliferous veins traverse the greenstone, pursuing a general course N. 50° to N. 65° E. They consist of quartz, with which are associated sulphate of barytes, spathic iron, and pyritiferous iron and copper. Gold has been found disseminated so abundantly through the vein-stones, that explorations upon them have been extensively carried on at times when mining operations were little in favor, capital not abundant ; and when the ores were necessarily transported several miles to the nearest mill.

The vein, which has been most worked, is traced

across a considerable portion of the Phœnix tract and the whole of the Vanderburg by a succession of pits sunk along its line of out-crop. On both tracts the mining upon it is now prosecuted to a depth requiring steam-power for the extraction of the water and ores. It has yielded rich bunches of gold ore near the surface ; and throughout the vein gold is diffused in such quantity, that the heaps of ore now lying upon the surface are valued at not less than $2.00 per bushel by the former proprietors of the Vanderburg mine. Many of the specimens extracted present a beautiful show of coarse gold, such as are not often found at the best mires in the State. As in depth the vein is more pyritiferous than near the surface, it is not unlikely the production may continue to greater depths than is usual at mines deficient in the yellow sulphurets of iron and copper. At Gold Hill, in the same vicinity, gold is abundant in the pyritiferous ores to the greatest depth yet reached, which is 340 feet. The deepest workings on the Vanderburg are only 100 feet. Pyritous copper ore is found in such quantity that the mine may fairly be regarded as a copper mine, and when further opened by lower levels than the present workings may reasonably be expected to produce largely of this ore. From my survey of the mine, sections of which accompany the map, it will be seen that the whole extent of the underground workings is only 176 feet, horizontally, and but a small portion of this is at the depth of the bottom of the shafts. With so great a length of vein the workings can be regarded as little more than superficial. The thickness of the vein varies from three and a half feet down to a few inches. It is more regular than the veins in Guilford County. It is remarkable for its smooth walls, and the "*comb*" like character of its vein-stones. This feature and the occurrence of the materials making the vein in parallel layers, which is also noticed here, are regarded by miners as very favorable signs of a good vein. Of itself this vein is sufficient to justify the establishment of mining operations on a liberal scale without reference to the other veins, some of which I now proceed to notice.

The next vein towards the South-east is eighteen rods distant, and pursues a course nearly parallel with the first, so far as it is exposed by the pits opened upon it. The material thrown out appears well as gold ore, and is encouraging for further exploration. The ground is favorably situated for opening the mine to advantage. As it can be proved for this reason, with little expense, it will be advisable to do this as soon as a mill is in operation for grinding the ores.

The third vein in this direction is called the "*Orchard* Vein:" having received this name on the Phœnix tract, from which it passes into the Vanderburg. It is on the latter about 83 rods South-east of the second vein just described. On the Phœnix its course is about N. 64° E. Approaching Plum Run it curves more to the Eastward, and its line of out-crop is very crooked. This is in part owing to the unevenness of the surface, which in connection with an underlay or dip to the N. W., somewhat

flat on the surface, would give greater irregularity of out-
line to the out-crop of a vein than belongs to its true
course. Many pits have been sunk along this vein
on the Vanderburg; a shaft also, from which a large
amount of material has been taken out, as is evident from
the size of the waste heap remaining; and a short adit
has been driven into the hill on the S. W. side of the
tract. On the Phœnix two shafts have been sunk upon
the same vein and a whim is now in operation working
it. My only means of forming an opinion of this vein
were—the general reputation it has; the extent of the
former operations, which corroborate its favorable repu-
tation; and the appearance of the stuff remaining upon
the surface. The rock forming the country is green-
stone with serpentine intermixed. The production of
gold, I learn from good authority, was considerable,
though the ore was of variable character. Pyritous cop-
per was met with in such quantity, both upon the Phœ-
nix and Vanderburg, that one would be well warranted
in sinking deep shafts in expectation of finding this ore
in abundance. In very superficial pits, at the workings
farther to the N. E., near the spring and large poplar,
noted upon the map, the indications of good copper are
very favorable, and here would be a convenient point for
sinking upon the vein, and taking off the surface water
by a short adit. Were a new Company to be organized
for working a portion of the mines of this tract, Plum
Run would make a convenient division and leave suf-
ficient territory to the South-east of it.

To the North-west of the first vein described, another vein of importance is found about fifty-seven rods distant. It has been worked on the lands of Julius Vanderburg, adjoining the Company's tract on the Northeast, by surface diggings and by a shaft forty feet deep. It is said to have produced good gold ore. On the other side the property, bordering the Phœnix Company's tract, the same vein (probably) out-crops on a little brook called Monkey Branch. Both gold and copper ores are here found loose in the banks of the stream; and, notwithstanding the prohibition of the former proprietor, the place has been with some a favorite resort after freshets for collecting little " nuggets " of gold. All applications for rights to wash the deposits have been steadily refused. From the information I gathered from one, who has been accustomed to the business of gold washing in this region, I am of opinion the vein along this part of Monkey Branch will be found a very valuable one; and the copper ores met with in the stream, which I found myself, are strong evidence of a workable vein of this metal.

" Branch mining," or working the deposits of the streams, has been prosecuted to a considerable extent in this region. A little run just over the boundary, in the farm of Julius Vanderburg, which crosses the continuation of the above-described vein, as also that of the vein now worked by the Company, has afforded a considerable amount of coarse gold. This fact, together with that of the veins, which must have furnished this deposit gold, being actually opened and presenting highly encouraging features, ought to inspire strong confidence, and lead to the laying out of mining operations on a scale commensurate with the extent and promise of the property. With a mill upon the spot for grinding the gold ores, the expense of transporting these, which is always a heavy item, is saved; and according to the extent of the mill, its capability of grinding up the poorer ores to profit in large quantities is increased, while the general expenses are reduced in proportion to the product. All mines furnish a much larger proportion of poor than rich ores. It is only those, which are extensively worked and provided with abundant machinery, than can make the great bulk of their products profitable. The difference in the returns must be very considerable, when only the ores yielding a dollar or more per bushel can be made to pay the expenses of preparation, and when those yielding twenty-five cents can be worked to profit, as is the case at some of the gold mines in Virginia. Few companies have so large a field for their operations, and one containing so many veins known to be productive as the Vanderburg Company.

Along the North-western boundary of the tract are pits sunk upon another vein. This may be a continuation of the " Faggot vein," which between these pits and the Hagler Lot (belonging to the Company) has been worked quite extensively. Several shafts were sunk upon this vein, beside almost a continuous line of pits up to the boundary of the Hagler Lot, which the vein enters upon its northern line. Running in a direction about S. 34° W., its course is obliquely across the longest dimensions of this lot. Separated from the nearest point of the main tract by only fifteen rods, this Hagler Lot of about 80 acres may be worked either under the same or a distinct organization.

The out-crop of still other veins is marked by loose pieces of quartz and other vein-stones near the eastern boundary of the main tract. These probably connect with the first and second veins described. Their position is noted upon the map, but no work having been done upon them, a particular description cannot be given.

Besides the Hagler Lot is another tract of about fifty-six acres lying near the main body of the property of the Company on the northern side of the farms of Julius Vanderburg and Tice Reinhardt. The nearest point of approach is 45 rods N. 62° 30' East of the extreme northern corner. Stretching thence to the eastward the lot takes the continuation of the veins, which pass through the centre of the main tract, and through the farm of J. Vanderburg. Several have been opened, and the extent of the pits upon no less than three of these veins indicate that here too they must have been found productive in gold. Although this tract may not be at once required for the operations of the Company, it cannot but be regarded as an important accession to their resources.

The "Plunkett" tract is a fourth lot about two miles distant, to the South-east, on a stream called Rock River.

This contains about ninety acres, and I am informed has upon it veins of similar character to the others in this region. My time was too limited to give this the same examination as the rest of the property,

With such resources—abundant territory well located, and containing numerous rivers, all producing gold and some copper ore also—the gold in many of the veins having heretofore, under disadvantageous circumstances, been extracted to profit, and the copper ores having every appearance of increasing in quantity and value as the mines are worked deeper—the property of the Vanderburg Mining Company is likely to repay generously the capital and enterprise expended in its thorough development.

Respectfully, I am yours, etc.,

JAMES T. HODGE.

CHARTER.

———

An Act to Incorporate the Excelsior Gold Mining Company in Cabarrus County

SEC. 1st. Be it enacted by the General Assembly of the State of North Carolina, and it is hereby enacted by the authority of the same : That WILLIAM P. FURNISS, WILLIAM FURNISS, and their associates, successors and assigns, are hereby created and constituted a body politic and corporate, by the name and style of the *Excelsior Gold Mining Company*, for the purpose of exploring and operating for gold and other metals, and minerals, and for mining, smelting and vending the same, and by that name and style, shall have all the rights and privileges of mining corporations in this State, and may purchase, hold and convey real and personal estate, not exceeding the value of one million of dollars.

SEC. 2d. Be it further enacted : That the first meeting of said Corporation may be called by the persons herein named, at such times and place as may be agreed upon by them, and at such and all other meetings legally notified ; said Corporation may make, alter or repeal such by-laws and regulations for the management of the business of said Corporation as a majority of the Stockholders may direct, not repugnant to the laws of this State and of the United States.

SEC. 3d. Be it further enacted : That the Capital Stock of said Company shall be two hundred and fifty thousand dollars, which may be divided into shares and sold and transferred in such manner and form as said Corporation may deem expedient ; and said Company may levy and collect assessments, forfeit and sell delinquent shares, declare and pay dividends in such manner as their by-laws may direct.

SEC. 4th. Be it further enacted : That one of the directors or officers of said Company shall always be a resident of Cabarrus County, and that service on him or any other director or officer of said Company shall be valued, and sufficient in law and equity for process or proceedings reasonable before any Judicial tribunal in this State, and it shall be the duty of the directors of said Company to have regular books of record and transfer kept by the Secretary or Treasurer thereof, at all times open to the inspection of the stockholders, or any one thereof.

SEC. 5th. Be it further enacted: That this Act shall be in force from and after its passage, and continue in force for the space of fifty years.

Read three times and ratified in General Assembly, this 16th day of February, 1855. SAM'L P. HILL, Speaker of the House of Commons; WARREN WINSLOW Speaker of the Senate.

* * * * * *
* SEAL. *
* * * * * *

STATE OF NORTH CAROLINA,
OFFICE SEC'Y OF STATE, *Raleigh, March* 16, 1874.

I hereby certify that the foregoing is a true copy of the original Act on file in this office.

WM. H. HOWESTON,

Secretary of State.

A REFRAIN.

I HOPE
I have not lost thee, Mary,
   I'm only thrust one side,
I had no prurient fantasie,
   To see thee as my bride.

'Twas a spirit that misled me,
   As thou knelt in silent prayer,
That an angel had descended,
   Through the dim, religious air

I was thinking of that Mary
   Whom Jesus loved as friend,
When sister Martha was so gary,
   And wouldn't stay to mend.

Thy dreamy gaze involved me,
   As I was passing down the aisle,
And its magic so dissolved me,
   That it made St. Clement smile.

A REFRAIN.

On a raining Sunday morning,
   As I sauntered in to prayers,
A messenger in sackcloth, mourning,
   Whispered slyly in my ears:

"Would you like to know Miss Teamy?"
   "Faith," says I, "I dinna care,"
It rather made me dreamy,
   With my usual debonnaire.

Then reflecting on the matter—
   For she looked so very sweet;
How the deuce was I to get at her,
   And contrive how we might meet?

Thus tempted with heard praises,
   Of her arts, and skill in look,—
For you know I love the Graces,—
   I discharged at her a book;

That was penned by Mistress Adams,
   Not she for poor Adam's ail,
The father of all those little dames
   That have made our race so "pale,"

Which, projected at my lassie,
   The subject of these verses,
Came back like coach, with glasses,
   Which follows solemn hearses.

I'm right sorry for the authoress,
   I thought only for her good,—
Case did not suit the doctoress;
   She needed better food.

But spring came with its verdure,
    With its shining coat of green,
And Astarte sent some flowers,
    The rarest to be seen.

And the patient had recovered
    From the offerings and the book,
But relapses were discovered,
    And of a serious turn partook.

'Twas an admiration offering only ;
    What's the harm in such a thing ?—
When the subject is a lady,
    And cat may look at king.

MORAL.

" Drink water out of your own cisterns, and running water out of your own wells."

" Cast thy bread upon the waters, and it shall return to thee after many days."

ON SEEING A BOUQUET OF FLOWERS IN A GLASS VASE.

Sweet flowers! so like the smiles from heaven,
  To brighten al. ur hours of toil,
Wherefrom the reapers gather leaven,
  Resting whilom from mid-day broil.

How well they ease the burthened heart,
  Too often wet with briny tears,
Quite comforting: where all was smart,
  The pains which blight and sorrow rears.

How joyfully ye kiss the dews
  That bathe your soft and lovely skin.
While rainbow prisms vie in hues,
  To paint your glory, without stint.

Ye blooming children from the skies,
  Earth-born, yet bursting out in praise;
In grateful incense ye do rise,
  To honor love, and joy, and grace.

How gladly, then, we view these flowers,
  So snugly nestled in a vase of glass,
The fairest image of the passing hours,
  Too soon to break and fade away, alas!

COL. O'BRIAN;

OR,

THE SOLDIER OF FORTUNE

BY ONE WHO KNEW HIM.

———◆———

ITZ O'BRIAN, of Irish descent, was a soldier of fortune, who, during the wars on the Spanish main, was engaged by the South Americans waging war against the rebels of that country. Noble, generous and brave, with a courage as indomitable as the lion, without fear and without reproach, he endeared himself to our countrymen, because he was a patriot and a true friend of all inclined to universal liberty.

He led the armies of the noble republics of that Southern land or continent, overcame the enemies of the government, and after a successful campaign, which ended in putting all the revolutionists to flight, laid down his arms to settle in glorious peace.

The government would have covered him with all the honors due to such braves, and they did indeed invest him with those paltry trinkets of gilt medals and the flaming insignia of titles, covered him with an emblazonry of gold lace, but could not hide his merit or virtues. He refused all compensation for his services, and spent all his patrimony of English gold freely as water or his own caprices suited. He was a gallant, bold, reckless and chivalrous man. Like Don Quixotte, he fought for the love of it. The gayest of soldiers, a true hearted, rollicking, rioting, frolicking Irishman, and as true to his honor as the dial to the sun.

I knew him well. I loved his hearty, free, rough-and-ready manner. There was a sparkle in his eyes, and sunshine in his laughter. He displayed his fun at all times, and was eccentric as he was bold and gifted, and he was gay.

Among the prospects, for he was somewhat of a speculative character, was his interests in a valuable silver mine, hid in the heart of the Andes, or it matters not where—say some part of Peru. This he offered to a friend for the privilege of working it, simply on the condition that he should pay all his debts, amounting to only about $15,000, a mere trifle and a cheap bargain for a mine which has yielded over $5,000,000 per annum.

The only risk attending the purchase would be, perhaps, the loss of the man's head who attempted to develop its treasures, and the fact that there needed a great deal of pumping before the water could be drawn out which had been overflowing the adits for a number of years back.

The history of this mine was rather singular. One Zalmanezer, a clever old Indian, had once been the owner of the property. It had been a gift from the empire for the many valuable services he had performed, but it was taken from him by one of those peculiar coups d' etats so common to despots, and concealed under the name of diplomatic tact, which sometimes compensates their most faithful servants by cutting off their heads. The influence of this aborignal was so great among his native subjects that government became jealous of him, and after having first baited him with the offer of a fee simple of this, his paramount estate of inheritance, accused him of tampering with the privities of royalty and the domains, and whilst he proffered a thousand dollars per day while he waited his answer to an appeal to the parent government in Spain, they refused his bail, against the action of the dishonorable and treacherous conduct on their part at home, and concluded that the best mode of getting rid of the popularity of a subject was to cut off his head, and thus control the entire right of possession.

Thus ever republics show their ingratitude. This is a solemn proverb and a warning; and like the farmer and his goose, they killed the bird in order to get her eggs. To remedy the short-sightedness exhibited in this picture of ingratitude, t .e companions of the Indian and his bosom friends, grateful and reminiscent of his many

friendly acts among the neighbors, very ingeniously con-
trived to pull out the plugs that had stopped the little
streams usually gushing out of the cavities in all mines
through the crevices and obstructing the proper working
of the laborers, and thus letting in a flood of water, burst
the sources of the neighboring lake and thereby destroyed
the schemes of the avaricious governor of Peru, and
thus placed a barrier to all future attempts to get this
silver.   Thus providence interrupts the course of human
monsters, and by a certain retribution puts a stop to the
evil as the beginning of complot.   Truly, " man proposes,
but God disposes."   " Vengeance is mine," saith the
Lord.   The poor Indian has become a constellation of
silver—in Heaven—by way of compensation.

But to return to our friend the Colonel.   He had va-
rious talents beside those of soldiering and gallant offi-
ces.   Not unskillful was he in the magic art of legerde-
main, and he often, among his circle of friends at the old
" stone arm chair," where he had built an abode, showed
them his tricks of slight of hand, which he had learned
while a youth at " Donnybrook Fair."

Here at this altar of festive repose he drank many a
bumper, and amid the sparkle of the wine and the brighter
flashes of his wit, our rollicking, frolicking and happy
Hibernian became green as the lizards on the Old Erin
Island whilst he rejoiced in his cups.   This art was learned
when he was poor, at home, and he went to the fair to
sharpen his wits for something to spend, like Curran, his
countryman, to whistle away the hunger.   Thus he lived

and after having frolicked and feasted, fought and played, he returned to the old country after having fought an arrant English officer who squinted too hard at one of his friend's sweethearts on board a man of war in the offing near Rio Janeiro.

The last we hear of him was after his return to Ireland, where he had expected to end his days. And in a racy letter to one of his early friends on the main he writes— " We have been up to the Lakes of Killarney, and it was nothing but swimming and hunting, hock and champagne."

SUMMER DAYS AT STOWE.

I.

Come, comrades, join your voices
  In song-before we go ;
The forest aisles will echoes ring,
  And bear the strains below.
As over us the moments pass,
  The moments lightly flow,
We'll sing, with praise of summer days,
  Of summer days in Stowe.

II.

'Neath the shadows of the mountains,
  Where the red man drew his bow,
We'll gather round the social board,
  And naught but pleasure know.
And when with reminiscences
  Our hearts are all aglow,
We'll sing, with praise of summer days,
  Of summer days in Stowe.

III.

Had this been Adam's Paradise
  Six thousand years ago,
No tempter e'er had entered in
  To fill the world with woe.
Eve would have sung her vesper hymn
  In cadence sweet and low,
As we sing now of summer days,
  Of summer days in Stowe.

IV.

Now, on the threshold of the night,
  Sol, lingering, bids us go,
And leave the homes of fairies bright
  Unvexed by foot of foe.
But let no chilling touch of time,
  While wandering to and fro,
Banish the thought of summer days,
  Of summer days in Stowe.

THE TOMB OF THE MARTYRS.

—

What hallowed associations are connected with the sound of martyrdom ! The heart of the patriot, the lover of his country, the true American, the honest man, and the sincere Christian, swells with emotions too deep for utterance. Great thoughts of heart arise in the bosom of all brave men, and noble women weep over the memories of the sacred dead :

"Dulce et decore est pro patriâ mori."

Adjoining the United States Navy Yard in Brooklyn city, in Jackson street, may be seen, in a dilapidate l condition, the tomb of the martyrs who died in dungeons and pestilential prison-ships, in and about the city of New York, during the seven years of our Revolutionary War.

What a disgrace to their living descendants, that the only monument that was ever erected to their memory should be suffered to remain in the sad and sorry plight in which it appears to-day !

It is high time that Brooklyn should wake up to a proper sense of their neglect of these departed worthies, and take the matter in hand, and rear a monument in some conspicuous spot, worthy of themselves, and which the children of future generations might visit, in order to keep alive and fresh their pride and honor for such patriotic exemplars. It would be a grand idea to mingle the bones of these heroes of the Revolution with those of the illustrious dead who have lately fought, bled, and died in our recent conflict against this last devilish Rebellion. Where rests your sense of shame, ye incorporators of Kings? Why have these ashes of your patriotic ancestors to be sanctified only by the colonists of New England; and why should the sapient wisdom of New Connecticut be called upon alone to place a statue over the buried martyrs in their vault and mouldering coffins at the purlieus of Wallabout? Why leave it to old Benjamin Romaine solely, as a monnment to his undying love and patriotism, and utter detestation of English impudence, to devise his body to the lot, in which these patriots have to inherit only their own bones, or to crown his pure devotion in a coronet of glory, which only exhibits thereon dark shadows in a strong contrast to the grim indifference of these Moabites of Long Island? Let the government lay hold of this matter, and sink their disgrace in a noble tribute to the memory of these glorious ancestors of our Independence! If they fail to do their duty, let us of Manhattan shame our neighbors on the other side of the East river into the doing of the correct thing in the present necessity. If these fail, let the spirit of the old Constitution itself, " that undying and perpetual charter of human rights, and of our duties to God and man," rise up like the bones of Elisha, which stood up on their feet at the indignant outrage of that band of wandering invaders, who, while casting only a very common man's corpse into the sepulchre of this venerable saint and prophet of old, plead that the dry bones of these modern vandals might shake in frightful

apprehension of that irrepressible disgrace and con-
tumely with which posterity will visit them for their
shameful neglect, and their remissful memories of the
past heroes of the Revolution, when it comes their turn
to be buried in vaults, and their ashes to be blown to
the winds in a tempest of tornadoes and tea-table talk
and reproach. Verily, the ashes of those dead patriots
are the embryo of the resurrection of our country ; and
we cannot better consecrate the ground where these
martyrs of the dust are buried so well as by raising
altars in the present on which the living may offer such
a savor of sweet incense as shall yield that consolation
and comfort of holy sacrifice, of thanksgiving, glory, and
praise, to heal the broken hearts of the widows and the
orphans, whose sorrows and wounds would be only
freshly opened, but for the recollection that the heroes
of the Revolution, and the honorable dead, brought forth
upon this *continent* a new nation, which was conceived
for the enjoyment of a greater liberty for all mankind,
which shall survive the wreck of empire and the fall of
kings, and shall endure only so long as we who are
alive shall honor their memories within the land which
the Lord our God has given us: It is but meet that we
dedicate a portion of our soil as the final resting-place
of those who gave their lives that this nation might live
forever. "*Requiescant in pace.*" Let us fi" up the
measure of their devotion. Amen.

A RAMBLE IN JULY,

A lady and a lassie and a lad,
  On a smiling July day,
Stepped out of the cars into Central Park,
  There happily to spend the day.

It was the first time in his life
  That the lad had seen the Ramble,
For he was led there like a little sheep,
  That had only just learned to gambol.

And ever as from little things a lesson we may learn,
  And from a small spark a great big fire may rise,
So it often seems that as troubled heart may burn,
  Should mortal from sepulchral earth be lifted to the skies.

Now we will change the age of him we called the lad,
  For men are but children first, but babes in later days,
And speaking boldly say 'twas a young man, be gad !
  Who was the first sad subject of these sorry lays.

It matters not even if a Red Rose of Lancaster
  Went with our party, she of maturer age,
As if one Pollox strayed away with Castor,
  'Twas all the worse for this little gentle page.

Nor makes it better that a white Rose of York,
  So sweetly smiled upon this youth forlorn,
For what's a smelling-bottle without its cork,
  Or what avails a valley without ripened corn ?

Secundo, we will change the nature of our metre—
  The day itself was changeable, as all fine weather is—
To ask the Muse to try a new gasometer,
  To let our gas off with a double whiz.

On a bright summer morning in the middle of July, the day
    As I was passing o'er the road, 'twas the 20th of July.
The sun was flirting with the clouds like hide-and-seek in play,
    When whom did I chance to meet but the idol of my eye.

'Twas very naughty of me, as you may well suppose,
    That such a man of business should be stopping by the way,
To cull a sweet white lily that was nestled near a Rose,
    Or to spend an hour by the fountain as it was dallying in its
       play.

The little golden diamonds that it scattered in the light
    Spread in starry shadows as it sparkled to the sun,
And my happy thoughts like violets bursting the night
    Of nursing mother earth, so inspired me I could not run.

We know the golden hours which were running like a stream,
    Though spent in sweet communion would ne'er return again
But the fountain and the flowers were weaving a sweet theme,
    Had been painted by the angels on Nature's wide domain.

It was of a stolen flower, that was pitcher-like in form,
    As it floated from its pendant, very like an ear-ring,
That one would have hardly thought of any harm,
    Or that there was aught of wrong in such a little thing.

But there ever was in stolen fruit a deal of mischief lurking,
    Even as where, in old Romaint, a maiden was stolen away
From her father's castellated halls, when gallant knight went
       burking
    And casting but a cloak around her, in his bark sped through
       the spray.

There never was since time of Eve, when Adam was away,
    But some de'il was there, to whisper slyly in the ear
There's something good in stealing, not, but there's the devi' to
       pay,
    And no harm that any ill will happen then to fear.

Now what shall be said when in another older saying
  You read that one cannot teach an old dog new tricks,
For even the elder lady pulled a sprig of jessamine, laying
  Not far from where a party sat on a bench of rustic sticks.

     " 'Twas ever thus, from childhood's hour,
       I've seen my fondest hopes decay;
     I never loved a tree or flower,
       But 'twas the first to fade away.
               "—Tom Moore."

Another poet, not so well read in verse,
  Doth now conclude this model prosaidy
By, never do write from railroad car, nor disperse
  Your thoughts from office calls—even for a lady.

        —

MORAL.

  Old Benjamin Franklin, so wise in his days,
  Was given to verses, but never to lays—
  'Twere a pity the moderns don't mind what he says,
  If they did, 'twould be surely more to their praise.

  Take care of the shop, and the shop will care for you;
  Always button your coat, and fasten your shoes,
  And then some fair lady will seek for a friend
  Who'll be true with her lover to life's bitter end.

CPSIA information can be obtained
at www.ICGtesting.com
Printed in the USA
BVHW041124150119
537879BV00009B/287/P